LB 2305 .E220 1988   Utley 15.⁰⁰

Entrepreneurship and Higher Education:
Lessons for Colleges, Universities, and Industry

by James S. Fairweather

ASHE-ERIC Higher Education Report No. 6, 1988

Media Center (Library)
ELIZABETHTOWN COMMUNITY COLLEGE
Elizabethtown, KY 42701

WITHDRAWN

D0024163

Prepared by

Clearinghouse on Higher Education
The George Washington University

Published by

Association for the Study of
Higher Education

Jonathan D. Fife,
Series Editor

Cite as

Fairweather, James S. *Entrepreneurship and Higher Education: Lessons for Colleges, Universities, and Industry.* ASHE-ERIC Higher Education Report No. 6. Washington, D.C.: Association for the Study of Higher Education, 1988.

Library of Congress Catalog Card Number 89-83629
ISSN 0884-0040
ISBN 0-913317-50-0

Managing Editor: Christopher Rigaux
Manuscript Editor: Barbara Fishel/Editech
Cover design by Michael David Brown, Rockville, Maryland

The ERIC Clearinghouse on Higher Education invites individuals to submit proposals for writing monographs for the Higher Education Report series. Proposals must include:
1. A detailed manuscript proposal of not more than five pages.
2. A chapter-by-chapter outline.
3. A 75-word summary to be used by several review committees for the initial screening and rating of each proposal.
4. A vita.
5. A writing sample.

ERIC **Clearinghouse on Higher Education**
School of Education and Human Development
The George Washington University
One Dupont Circle, Suite 630
Washington, D.C. 20036-1183

ASHE **Association for the Study of Higher Education**
Texas A&M University
Department of Educational Administration
Harrington Education Center
College Station, Texas 77843

This publication was prepared partially with funding from the Office of Educational Research and Improvement, U.S. Department of Education, under contract no. ED RI-88-062014. The opinions expressed in this report do not necessarily reflect the positions or policies of OERI or the Department.

EXECUTIVE SUMMARY

Higher education and industry enter the 1990s with strong incentives to form alliances. The combination of academic leaders in search of revenue, industrialists looking for a competitive edge, and state and federal governments attempting to restore economic vitality has resulted in dramatic growth in industry-university liaisons. Advocates claim that these liaisons are inevitable, either because refocusing academic resources toward economic needs is needed to restore the economy and benefit society (Public Policy Center 1986) or because to compete effectively for faculty, students, and research funds, academic institutions currently without strong ties with industry must copy the behavior of institutions that pursue such ties.

Yet questions remain about the impact of partnerships between business and higher education, both for participants and for society. Some opponents of these collaborative agreements claim that moving from basic research and instruction toward product development and marketing reduces the contribution of academe to society and, in the long run, threatens economic vitality (Caldert 1983). Others question the ability of colleges and universities to foster economic growth through liaisons with industry.

Little evidence exists to support either claims of effectiveness or predictions of dire consequences (Feller 1988). The crucial questions remain unanswered: Will industry-university liaisons change academic institutions in ways that increase social and economic benefits? Are industry-university connections cost-effective vehicles for enhancing economic development? Will academic-industrial partnerships be another in a long line of educational fads, leaving little imprint on the social fabric?

To assist government, industrial, and academic leaders, this monograph analyzes the existing literature to provide a framework for examining industry-university relationships and for evaluating their impact on a variety of social, economic, and educational goals. The first section describes the emergence of industry-university liaisons, the next four discuss ideological agendas, motivating forces, characteristics and typologies of liaisons, and operational issues, two subsequent sections discuss the compatibility of business–higher education partnerships with academic functions and the assessment of impact and effectiveness, and the final one elaborates lessons for academic, corporate, and governmental decision makers.

Whose Ideology, Yours or Mine?

Ideological positions often guide the debate about relationships between business and higher education. These positions, which are influenced by beliefs about the nature of academic institutions and their role in society, range from strong advocacy to outright opposition. Advocates believe the university should play an active role in economic development through such activities as continuing professional education, technology transfer, and product development. Opponents of industry-university liaisons either believe that the contributions of universities result from its independence from the marketplace or are not convinced that academic institutions are effective vehicles for enhancing economic growth. Regardless of ideological position, the lack of interest in considering or calculating the costs and benefits of industry arrangements to academic institutions.and the concomitant lack of evaluative data are striking.

What Is the Motivation for Forming Partnerships?

State and federal governments promote alliances between business and higher education to enhance economic competitiveness. The focus is on resolving the trade imbalance, increasing productivity, ensuring that university research meets the needs of industry, and promoting the commercialization of knowledge gained through research.

Similarly, industries form liaisons with academic institutions to improve their competitive position. The most important benefits are access to graduates and to faculty expertise and upgraded training of staff, but enhanced innovation and product development are also important.

In considering liaisons with industry, academic institutions are primarily motivated by financial need. Industry is a source of potential direct revenue. Forming relationships with industry is also an indirect mechanism for demonstrating responsiveness to state economic development agendas, which might result in enhanced state funding of academic institutions. Other considerations focus on faculty and student needs, prestige, and public relations.

What Types of Industry-University Liaisons Have Been Formed?

The most visible alliances between business and higher education are research agreements between large corporations and prominent academic institutions. These arrangements account for a large portion of funds given to academic institutions by industry but for only a small portion of relationships between them. Additional types of liaisons include research agreements with individual faculty, donations and contributions, and education and training programs. Other four- and two-year institutions participate in many of these latter relationships.

Industry has concentrated its funding of academic institutions in a few technical fields of particular importance to the corporate sponsor—engineering, computer science, medicine, agriculture, chemistry, and, more recently, biotechnology.

What Does It Take to Form a Liaison?

Industry and academe differ fundamentally in motivation, goals, organizational structures, and employee attitudes and behavior. Resolution of these differences is crucial to establishing and operating industry-university relationships. Keys to successful implementation include previous experience working with industry or academe, demographic characteristics (proximity, size, financial health, capacity for research and development, product line/discipline), overlap of needs, leadership, mutual understanding of cultures and missions, resolution of potential conflicts with academic freedom, and high probability of benefits. Keys to successful operation include flexibility of the academic organizational structure, sufficient capacity and resources, and match of the arrangement with the academic reward structure and faculty workloads.

Is the Arrangement Compatible with Academe?

The compatibility of industry-university relationships with academic institutions of higher education varies by function. For research and scholarship, the potential benefits of liaisons with industry are enhanced resources and improved facilities. The potential financial costs center on whether the additional revenue generated exceeds the additional administrative costs and institutional subsidies required by forming liaisons with industry. Other potential costs include threats to academic freedom, less open exchange of information, disputes over intellectual property rights, and exacerbating the split between the haves and the have nots (Blumenthal et al. 1986).

For instruction, the potential benefit of alliances between business and higher education is improved ability to recruit students and faculty. The potential costs include decreased emphasis on undergraduate education, conflict with doctoral program processes, reduced faculty attention to instruction, and lessened student-faculty interaction (Fairweather n.d.).

Industry-university relationships that emphasize continuing education seem compatible with the function of academic service. Relationships that focus on technology transfer and economic development, especially those that emphasize product development, creation of spinoff companies, and university-formed for-profit ventures, may conflict with academic freedom and adversely affect the faculty workload.

The larger question of compatibility concerns the overall impact of industry-university liaisons on the academic institution. Relevant concerns include the type of institution that results from pursuit of economic development, whether or not this evolution is effective, and whether the benefits outweigh the costs. Assessment of overall impact is complex because a single relationship can simultaneously enhance certain academic functions while harming others.

What Lessons Can Academic, Corporate, and Government Leaders Learn?

1. *The nature of science and innovation.* The transition from idea to product is not straightforward: Many technical innovations have resulted from research carried out without commercial application in mind. High expectations for direct economic benefits from industry-university liaisons, especially in the short term, are unrealistic.
2. *The myth of generalizability.* Despite their widespread appeal, only a few corporations and universities have the resources and expertise for large-scale research liaisons.
3. *The match between capacity and goals.* The key to any industry-university relationship is the match between capacity and capability, on the one hand, and the goals and purposes of the liaison, on the other. The diversity of industry-university relationships makes this calculation difficult. In relationships involving technology transfer, for example, determining the match between capacity and goals must take into account whether a particular liaison relies on faculty and graduate students to assist industry or whether it relies on non-tenure-track research staff to play these roles.
4. *Academic policy.* Formulation of institutional policy can ensure the preservation of academic goals more effec-

tively than leaving faculty and department heads to strike their own bargains.

5. *The importance of structure.* Beyond administrative convenience, the location of an industrially funded project in a college or university can reinforce academic functions by affecting faculty members' behavior. For example, placement in an interdisciplinary research unit might reinforce project research goals but decrease faculty involvement in instruction and service. Placement in a' department might reinforce instructional goals but be less effective for research. In either case, the location has associated costs and benefits beyond the confines of the research agreement.

6. *Preserving distinctiveness and identity.* Maintaining some distance from market forces has allowed academic institutions to retain expertise and capacity in fields that might emerge again years later. If universities had closed their engineering schools when few engineers could find jobs, for example, the American economy would be in much worse shape today.

Above all, universities should retain the capacity to do what no other organization does as well—namely, provide a broad liberal education for the populace, train future professionals, and combine research and instruction in the search for knowledge. Relationships with industry that enhance other goals without harming these basic functions may prove beneficial. The social costs of industry-university relationships that diminish the capacity of academic institutions to address fundamental, distinctive missions may exceed the sum of their benefits, however.

ADVISORY BOARD

Roger G. Baldwin
Assistant Professor of Education
College of William and Mary

Carol M. Boyer
Senior Policy Analyst for Higher Education
Education Commission of the States

Clifton F. Conrad
Professor of Higher Education
Department of Educational Administration
University of Wisconsin–Madison

Elaine H. El-Khawas
Vice President
Policy Analysis and Research
American Council on Education

Martin Finkelstein
Associate Professor of Higher Education Administration
Seton Hall University

Carol Everly Floyd
Associate Vice Chancellor for Academic Affairs
Board of Regents of the Regency Universities System
State of Illinois

George D. Kuh
Professor of Higher Education
School of Education
Indiana University

Yvonna S. Lincoln
Associate Professor of Higher Education
University of Kansas

Richard F. Wilson
Associate Chancellor
University of Illinois

Ami Zusman
Principal Analyst, Academic Affairs
University of California

CONSULTING EDITORS

Charles Adams
Director, The Inquiry Program
Center for the Study of Adult and Higher Education
University of Massachusetts

Ann E. Austin
Research Assistant Professor
Vanderbilt University

Trudy W. Banta
Research Professor
University of Tennessee

Robert J. Barak
Deputy Executive Secretary
Director of Academic Affairs and Research
Iowa Board of Regents

Robert Berdahl
Professor of Higher Education
University of Maryland

Kenneth A. Bruffee
Director, The Scholars Program
Brooklyn College of the City University of New York

L. Leon Campbell
Provost and Vice President for Academic Affairs
University of Delaware

Ellen Earle Chaffee
Associate Commissioner for Academic Affairs
North Dakota State Board of Higher Education

Robert Paul Churchill
Chair and Associate Professor
Department of Philosophy
George Washington University

Charles S. Claxton
Associate Professor
Center for the Study of Higher Education
Memphis State University

Susan Cohen
Associate, Project for Collaborative Learning
Lesley College

Peter T. Ewell
Senior Associate
National Center for Higher Education Management Systems

Irwin Feller
Director, Institute for Policy Research and Evaluation
Pennsylvania State University

Reynolds Ferrante
Professor of Higher Education
George Washington University

Zelda F. Gamson
Director
New England Resource Center for Higher Education

Milton Greenberg
Provost
American University

Judith Dozier Hackman
Associate Dean
Yale University

Paul Jedamus
Professor
University of Colorado

Lynn G. Johnson
Executive Director
Hudson-Mohawk Association of Colleges and Universities

Oscar T. Lenning
Vice President for Academic Affairs
Robert Wesleyan College

Charles J. McClain
President
Northeast Missouri State University

Judith B. McLaughlin
Research Associate on Education and Sociology
Harvard University

Marcia Mentkowski
Director of Research and Evaluation
Professor of Psychology
Alverno College

Richard I. Miller
Professor, Higher Education
Ohio University

James R. Mingle
Executive Director
State Higher Education Executive Officers

James L. Morrison
Professor
University of North Carolina

Elizabeth M. Nuss
Executive Director
National Association of Student Personnel Administrators

Anne M. Pratt
Director for Foundation Relations
College of William and Mary

Karen T. Romer
Associate Dean for Academic Affairs
Brown University

Jack E. Rossmann
Professor of Psychology
Macalester College

Donald M. Sacken
Associate Professor
University of Arizona

Robert A. Scott
President
Ramapo College of New Jersey

J. Fredericks Volkwein
Director of Institutional Research
State University of New York at Albany

William R. Whipple
Director, Honors Program
University of Maine

CONTENTS

FOREWORD

The thought of close ties between institutions of higher education and industry has been greeted with both derision and acclaim. Whether one finds this threatening or sees institution/industry relations as visionary, there is increased external and internal pressure to move in this direction. To avoid disappointment, planners must understand both the liabilities and assets in such relations.

Three primary reasons given for institutions *not* to develop close relationships with industry are:

- a fear that academic freedom and the ability to freely discuss and publish new discoveries will be stifled under the need for corporate proprietary secrecy;
- a fear from the faculty that such relationships will drain money away from other missions of the institution, especially teaching in the less commercially viable areas; and
- a fear of political backlash from state legislators if short-term economic expectations are not met.

Among the compelling arguments in support of entrepreneurial relations between college and industry are:

- increased faculty awareness to "real world" problems;
- improved access by faculty and students to cutting-edge technology, especially in scientific and technical areas, which cannot be developed internally because of current institutional financial constraints;
- access to industry personnel, which can be used to augment their teaching faculty;
- enhanced institutional revenue by the commercialization of faculty research discoveries;
- presumed improved stature and funding for state-supported institutions that demonstrate a positive connection between institutional research activities and the state's economy.

In order to avoid disappointment and to maximize opportunity in college/industry relationships, institutions need to analyze carefully what they realistically can expect to deliver. Conversely, they need to assess realistically what they can expect to receive from industry, both in short- and long-term benefits. In this report, James Fairweather of the Pennsylvania State University provides a comprehensive framework for analyzing the pros and cons of engaging in entrepreneurial relationships.

As the rewards are great, so too the risks are apparent and should not be minimized. However, proper planning and attention to detail can enable most institutions to avoid the pitfalls and achieve a beneficial relationship with selected organizations. What should not be excused is a refusal to consider this important issue with the due consideration it deserve.

Jonathan D. Fife
Professor and Director
ERIC Clearinghouse on Higher Education
School of Education and Human Development
The George Washington University

ACKNOWLEDGMENTS

Two graduate students, Dennis Brown and Phillip Feerrar, assisted in the bibliographic search in preparing this monograph. I value their assistance, both professionally and in terms of emotional support. I also appreciate the support of my colleagues at Penn State, both faculty and students. Roger Geiger in particular was helpful. I appreciate the editorial comments from the external reviewers. And I thank my wife, Linda, whose enduring patience made it possible for me to complete the work.

THE EMERGENCE OF INDUSTRY-UNIVERSITY LIAISONS

The 1980s might be called the decade of the "industry-university liaison" or the "business-university partnership." The combination of academic leaders searching for needed revenues, industrialists looking for a renewed competitive edge, and state and federal governments attempting to restore economic vitality has resulted in dramatic growth in these relationships and in advocacy for them. Yet questions remain about the impact of partnerships between business and higher education, both for participants and for society. Will industry-university liaisons change academic institutions in ways that increase social and economic benefits? Will colleges and universities (and perhaps industry) evolve in ways not beneficial to society? Are industry-university connections cost-effective vehicles for enhancing economic development? Will academic-industrial partnerships be another in a long line of educational fads, leaving little imprint on the social fabric?

This monograph examines the existing literature to provide a framework for examining corporate-university relationships and for assessing their impact on a variety of social, economic, and educational goals. This section examines the emergence of industry-university liaisons, including a historical perspective of corporate support for higher education, a review of the social and educational forces in the 1980s that have combined to modify the nature of relationships between business and higher education, and a discussion of the potential costs and benefits of these relationships.

To better understand industry-university liaisons, the next four sections discuss various ideological agendas, motivating forces, characteristics and typologies of liaisons, and operational issues; to examine the impact of these liaisons, two subsequent sections discuss the compatibility of business–higher education partnerships with academic functions and the assessment of impact and effectiveness. The final section elaborates lessons for academic, corporate, and governmental decision makers.

The crux of the argument is whether the changes resulting from partnerships with industry negate the very practices, activities, and culture that have produced such magnificent scientific and technical breakthroughs in the past.

Historical Patterns

Corporate support for academe is not new; it originated at the beginning of the 20th century (Hutt 1983, p. 107). Private contributions to academic research started in the 1920s (Dickson 1984; Geiger 1988). Cooperation between industry and higher education was stimulated by the Morrill Act of 1862, which created land-grant institutions to focus on applied research and service to society (Johnson 1984, pp. 15–17), the two world wars, and the creation of federal agencies like the National Science Foundation to fund research (Geiger 1988; Johnson 1984).

Concern about the effect of external funding, including funds from industry, on academe also are not new. The potential influence of external funding on academic freedom and other academic activities long has been recognized as a potential problem. To conduct research of any significance, universities have had to seek funding from a variety of external sources (Geiger 1988). This dependence conflicts with the concept of the ivory tower espoused by many leading academics:

> *The universities have demonstrated their willingness to do almost anything for money. Government and business are not wholly disinterested in their approaches to the universities; they are not seeking the truth, but are hiring universities to promote the ends they have in view. If the truth serves these ends, it is merely a coincidence* (Hutchins 1962, pp. x–xi).

From this perspective, the negative consequences for academe apply equally to federally and industrially funded research (National Science Foundation 1982b, p. 4; Price 1965, p. 17).

The 1980s and the Rise of Industry-University Liaisons

Although corporate support for higher education has significant historical roots, the 1980s have evidenced an evolution (perhaps revolution) in the types of relationships and extent of the support. Two principal causes underlie these changes: radically different American and world economies and additional factors affecting colleges and universities quite independent from economic issues.

Changing nature of the economy

The past two decades have evidenced a shift from an industrial to an information economy (Bell 1973, 1979; Botkin, Dimancescu, and Strata 1982). Accompanying this shift has been a dramatic increase in the rate of technological change, the internationalization of the economy, and increased competitiveness (Kreps 1986). The competitiveness of American industry in the world economy has diminished, creating the perception of a national economic crisis (Hatsopoulos, Krugman, and Summers 1988):

The traditional industrial base has eroded, creating a need for alternative policies to assist "rust belt" states in diversifying their economies. The United States no longer dominates the production of high-technology goods nor the technical disciplines that underlie this production. Instead, Japan, Korea, and others are actively competing for leadership in the forthcoming technologically oriented economy (Fairweather n.d.).

The "new economy" differs from the industrial economy in several ways. Industry is required to invest more heavily in research and development and to take a longer-term view toward profit (Choate 1986, p. 14). Most new jobs are now located in small businesses and technology-based companies rather than in large manufacturing corporations (Swanson 1986, p. 24). Human capital has become central to the information economy (Hersh 1983, p. 6), a concept that includes addressing manpower shortages in key fields; providing enhanced technical training for the work force; enhancing literacy, remediation, and training in basic skills; and addressing the underrepresentation of women and minorities (Public Policy Center 1986; Smith 1986, p. 65).

Views about the process of innovation also have changed. Traditionally, innovation was seen as a linear process with clearly distinguished roles. Basic research was the domain of the university. Findings from basic research led to applied research, which led eventually to development, marketing, and dissemination (Bush 1945; Noble 1977).

The linear model has been found inadequate. Experience shows that innovation is not linear—nor are roles always clearly distinguishable. For example, although colleges and universities account for the majority of expenditures for basic research (48 percent), industry also contributes significantly (20 percent). Similarly, industry accounts for most of the expenditures for applied research (65 percent), but academic contributions are also significant (11 percent). As expected, industry dominates expenditures for product development (National Science Board 1987, pp. 77–78).

Another change in attitude toward the process of innovation concerns the length of time required to translate university-based basic research into a useful product. In the past, this process has been characterized as too slow to benefit the economy:

When the use of basic research findings in industry involves a gap of up to twenty years, it is moot whether one can speak of a university-industry interaction in any meaningful sense (Johnson and Tornatzky 1981, p. 48).

More recently, industrial and academic leaders have come to consider the time period between basic research and product development as considerably shorter.

Factors affecting higher education
Institutions of higher education are perceived as relatively slow to respond to changes in the economic environment. This criticism is particularly aimed at public universities, which incorporate public service as one of their missions (Dressel 1987). In all postsecondary institutions, the responsibilities for transmission of culture, preparation of educated citizens, training of professionals, and production of knowledge through scholarly research coexist uneasily, often conflicting within a single institution (Bowen and Schuster 1986; Boyer 1987; Cole 1982; Geiger 1986; Study Group 1984). Exacerbating this conflict are *institutional perspectives*, which focus on campus responsibilities, and *disciplinary perspectives*, where faculty are driven by the concerns of disciplinary peers often outside their own institutions (Alpert 1985). Over time, these conflicts of organization, perspective, and mission have resulted in an "alarming disintegration of consensus about purpose" (Ashby 1971, p. 4), "especially about the *relative importance* of the varied higher education functions in society" (Fairweather n.d.).

Land-grant institutions especially have been criticized for their lack of responsiveness to social and economic needs:

The pervasive attitude in our land-grant universities [is] that applied work is not important; publishing for professional peers and consulting for the highest-paying firm or government agency are the priority tasks (Schuh 1986, p. 6).

The single-minded emphasis on "moving up the prestige ladder" and the focus of the academic reward structure on research and scholarship have reinforced this perceived refusal to address societal needs adequately (Alpert 1985; Bowen and Schuster 1986, p. 150; Schuh 1986, p. 6). Some critics have called for the renewal of university participation in society akin to that envisioned in the original Morrill Act of 1862 (Diman-cescu and Botkin 1986, p. 12; Schuh 1986, p. 6).

Concern also has been raised about the perceived decline in the quality of higher education programs. Several eminent aca-demicians have called for improvements in undergraduate in-struction (Bowen and Schuster 1986; Boyer 1987; Cole 1982; National Science Board 1986; Study Group 1984). Others are concerned about the stabilization and in some cases decline in resources made available to postsecondary institutions (Bok 1982; Boyer 1987; Business–Higher Education Forum 1984). Of special concern is the decline in real dollars of federal con-tributions to academic research (National Science Foundation 1984a, 1985d), which has affected the quality of laboratory fa-cilities and equipment and academic programs (Mai 1984; Na-tional Research Council 1985b, pp. 21–22; Peters and Fusfeld 1983):

> *What these data imply is that for the past 10 years the insti-tutions of higher education have been balancing their budget by omitting certain desirable expenditures. . . . The critical question is the character and impact of these omitted expen-ditures: To the extent that they were inefficiencies, budget "fat," or unnecessary frills, the tight budget situation pro-vided a desirable result; to the extent that they involved the elimination of essential programs, reduced the effectiveness of instruction and research, or otherwise affected adversely the quality of education is clearly a matter for concern. An examination of the facts suggests strongly that the omissions have fallen much more in the latter category than in the for-mer* (Business–Higher Education Forum 1984, p. 8).

The new infrastructure

For·many parties, these forces have combined to change the view of academe as a passive contributor to the economy, prin-cipally through the training of students, toward the perception of the university as an active resource in redressing economic ills (Bach and Thornton 1983; Business–Higher Education Forum 1984; "Business and Universities" 1982; David 1982; Dickson 1984; Feller 1986; Johnson 1984; Kenney 1986; Lyn-ton and Elman 1987; Mai 1984; Peters and Fusfeld 1983; Pub-lic Policy Center 1986). Given the educational orientation of the evolving economy, including the need for enhanced human capital and for research and development, many argue that the view of academe as a detached entity is no longer sufficient (Chmura, Henton, and Melville 1988; Cross 1981; Dimancescu and Botkin 1986; Kreps 1986; Lynton and Elman 1987; Public Policy Center 1986):

From this viewpoint, universities must shift from the accumulation and interpretation of basic knowledge toward active dissemination and provision of technical assistance; that is, academe should be responsive to the various external clients interested in the knowledge generated by university faculty and staff (Fairweather n.d.).

Industry-university relationships

Public-private partnerships increasingly have become the vehicle of choice for promoting economic growth, whether through technology transfer or the creation of new technical companies (Brooks 1984, p. 10). Industry-university liaisons are an important subset of public-private partnerships, advocated in both the United States and its international competitors: Belgium (Declerq 1979), Canada (Buchbinder and Newson 1985), China (Bernstein 1986), France (Bernstein 1986), the Federal Republic of Germany (U.S. Department of Commerce 1980), Great Britain (Bernstein 1986; MacKenzie and Rhys Jones 1985; Michel 1985), and Japan (U.S. Department of Commerce 1980).

Federal agencies have encouraged links between industry and institutions of higher education through grants and contracts (National Research Council 1985b; National Science Board 1986; National Science Foundation 1982b; Praeger and Omenn 1980).

Various organizations and institutions are developing programs (such as the Semiconductor Research Corporation and the National Science Foundation's Engineering Research Centers) designed to foster closer ties between engineering colleges and industry. More such creative and innovative programs of a specific nature are needed to strengthen the bond between engineering schools and industry (National Research Council 1985b, pp. 13–14).

State governments also have encouraged increased ties between business and higher education (Chmura, Henton, and Melville 1988; Public Policy Center 1986; Watkins 1985). The

Ben Franklin Partnership in Pennsylvania, as one of many examples, encourages universities to work with industry to form new companies, increase employment, and improve the transfer of technology (Corporation for Penn State 1986; Lynton and Elman 1987).

The underlying philosophy is that industry-university collaboration can enhance the competitiveness of the American economy (Bach and Thornton 1983; National Research Council 1985b, pp. 13–14; National Science Board 1986, pp. 4–5). This viewpoint has become dominant in many government, industry, and academic circles:

> *Overall, reservations concerning the appropriateness or effectiveness of closer [industry-university] collaboration have been tabled in the present period of "positive sum" aspiration, specter of long-term economic decline, and programmatic advocacy* (Feller 1988, p. 2).

The academic-industrial response. Universities and industry have responded to these pressures. Between 1982 and 1985, the number of research and development consortia between industry and academic institutions increased five times (Dimancescu and Botkin 1986); almost all of the major industry-university research consortia were established since 1979 (Dimancescu and Botkin 1986; Fowler 1984, p. 38). A 1982 study found that one-half of 463 industry-university relationships actively working in 1982 were new within three years (Peters and Fusfeld 1983, p. 20), and a 1986 survey of 300 four-year postsecondary institutions indicated that 97 percent plan to initiate activities related to economic development (Public Policy Center 1986, p. ix).

Although contributing only 6 percent of the total, industry is the fastest-growing source of support for academic research and development. The contributions from industry rose from $40 million in 1960 to $670 million in 1987 (National Science Board 1987, pp. 78, 243–44). The top 28 research universities have doubled the research funds received from industry in the past decade (Geiger 1988). Other indications of greater collaboration include increases in articles authored jointly by academic and industrial scientists; universities' pursuit of patents; long-term industrially funded academic research; universities' pursuit of industrial funding; organizational arrangements for research; and funding targeted for industry-university partnerships by federal, state, and local governments (Geiger 1988; National Science Board 1987).

Unclear boundaries. The response by business and higher education has not been limited to joint relationships. Each has pursued economic development independently, resulting in a less distinct boundary between academe and industry.

One such area is education and training, which no longer is the distinct province of the universities:

> *Life on the frontier is of necessity going to be more interactive for education providers. Formerly parallel paths are already merging and intersecting and in general behaving in thoroughly unparallel ways* (Cross 1981, p. 6).

In-house corporate education and training is now a major force in postsecondary education, receiving about the same investment as all of higher education (Aslanian and Brickell 1981, p. 18; Craig and Evers 1981; Eurich 1985, p. 6). In addition, interactive vehicles like college apprenticeship programs further blur the boundaries between academe and industry. An automotive mechanics program, for example, might be offered by both a community college and a local company (Gold 1981, pp. 14–15). And at least 18 corporations now offer degree-granting programs in separate institutes, including the Rand Graduate Institute, the Arthur D. Little Management Education Institute, the G.M.I. Engineering and Management Institute, the DeVry Institute of Technology, the National Technological University, and the Wang Institute of Graduate Studies (Eurich 1985, pp. 88–95).

These trends are reinforced by the change in the flow of human resources. The traditional path from college to work no longer dominates patterns of enrollment. Instead, new patterns are characterized by adult learners returning to school after participating in the work force and by practicing professionals receiving additional training while working (Gold 1981, pp. 16–17).

The overlap is not limited to industry's mimicking academe; several universities have formed companies to develop and market products. In biotechnology, as one example, entrepreneurship by academic institutions and faculty is accepted and encouraged (Culliton 1981; Kenney 1986; Wofsy 1986).

Complementary or Conflicting?

The overlap of activities, initiation of partnerships, and occasional competition between academic institutions and industry mask a more subtle shift toward similar behavior and objectives:

> The current patterns, and certainly the trend-setting innovations, go far beyond cooperative partnerships between business and colleges: They reflect the adoption of similar objectives; the overlapping of functions; the copying of organizational structures; the appointment of counterpart personnel; the emergence of colleges as companies, companies as colleges; and the proliferation of academic corporations and corporate colleges (Aslanian and Brickell 1981, p. 18).

Are such changes desirable? Despite increased support for alliances between business and higher education, some observers caution that the costs of such liaisons to universities and to society may exceed any direct economic benefit ("Business and Universities" 1982, p. 58; Kenney 1986, p. 31). The crux of the argument is whether the changes resulting from partnerships with industry negate the very practices, activities, and culture that have produced such magnificent scientific and technical breakthroughs in the past (Association of American Universities 1986, p. 39; Caldert 1983, p. 25; Culliton 1981, p. 1195):

> To maintain watchful concern for the health of these relatively few institutions [i.e., research universities] does not require blindness to their faults or unrelieved admiration for all of their works, only a sense of how extraordinary it is to have a set of institutions whose net social value is so great and how difficult it is to repair serious damage to them (Rosenzweig and Turlington 1982, pp. 1–2).

Among the areas of concern are threats to institutional autonomy and academic freedom, including choice of research topic and open distribution of research results (Caldert 1983, p. 27). Some commentators argue that academic freedom is related to the substantial social benefits derived from academic research; threats to academic freedom might be counterproductive to economic development (Rosenzweig and Turlington 1982, p. 6). Others argue that the apparent merging of academic and industrial interests through various administrative arrangements is illusory; academic and corporate values must at their heart always conflict:

> *The complementary nature of these [industry-university] activities, however, simply throws into relief the basic difference between universities and industry: the academic imperative to seek knowledge objectively and to share it openly and freely; and the industrial imperative to garner a profit, which frequently creates the incentive to treat knowledge as private property* (Giamatti 1983, p. 5).

A proposal in the early 1980s to establish a for-profit genetics engineering corporation at Harvard University summarizes the pros and cons of academic-industrial connections. The proposal eventually was rejected but the appeal of the arrangement was substantial and the eventual outcome left in doubt. The proposal was rejected because of concerns:

> *(1) that academic discussion could be impaired because of commercial competition; (2) that professors and graduate students might shirk academic duties and interests to pursue commercial ones; (3) that the administration's authority to protect its academic interests might diminish; and (4) that Harvard's reputation for academic integrity might be damaged by even the appearance of conflict between its academic and financial interests. The university administration emphasized, however, that it badly needed additional sources of funding to strengthen the university's teaching and research and that it would continue to explore similar proposals* (Weiner 1982, p. 87).

Indeed, in subsequent years Harvard actively has promoted the use of limited partnerships for the commercialization of results of biological and pharmaceutical research.

Who is right, the advocates or the opponents? The cautious advocates, who argue for careful management of industry-university alliances while supporting the goals of these relationships? The cautious opponents, who argue for close monitoring of existing liaisons while opposing new initiatives? Is a situational solution the answer: industry-university partnerships work under specific conditions but not others? Given the respective problems of increased competitiveness and declining resources, can industry and universities be expected to behave in ways other than those encouraged by proponents of partnerships?

These questions are not easy to answer. The literature is devoted to anecdotal success stories; failures are seldom described, making comparative analyses difficult (Feller 1986, 1988; Long and Feller 1972; Nelson 1982). Moreover, the literature is dominated by philosophical arguments and disagreements; the lack of evaluative data is glaring (Bach and Thornton 1983, p. 31). And little evidence exists to indicate whether industry-university alliances actually produce cost-effective economic benefits.

At this point, the best approach is to increase our understanding of the motivations for forming partnerships and of the different formats of academic-industrial liaisons. Data suggesting the extent to which these liaisons might affect academe, industry, and economic development also are useful, as is an elaboration of alternative mechanisms for assessing industry-university partnerships. This preparatory information is crucial to making recommendations for academic, corporate, and government leaders concerning industry-university relationships.

IDEOLOGICAL AND POLITICAL AGENDAS

Little evidence exists to support or contradict claims about the effectiveness or impact of the newer industry-university research relationships. The little data available on the outcomes of these relationships raise questions about their cost-effectiveness for universities (Blumenthal, Epstein, and Maxwell 1986) and about the ability of academic institutions to enhance the competitiveness of industry (Slaughter n.d.; Stankiewicz 1986). Even descriptive data are limited. Of the literature reviewed for this monograph, 12 works could be classified as descriptive studies (Brazziel 1981a, 1981b; Burdette 1988; Chmura 1987; Day 1985; Fowler 1984; Haller 1984; Johnson and Tornatzky 1984; Larsen and Wigand 1987; National Science Foundation 1982b; Peters and Fusfeld 1983; Zinser 1982). An additional four are research-based legal analyses (Fowler 1982–83; Hutt 1983; Reams 1986; Tatel and Guthrie 1983). In addition to annual reports from spinoff companies, which might contain data useful in evaluating industry-university partnerships (e.g., Corporation for Penn State 1986), only eight studies directly examined effectiveness, impact, and other outcomes. For three of these "evaluations," the links between data gathered, analyses, and recommendations are unclear (Dimancescu and Botkin 1986; Kenney 1986; Public Policy Center 1986), making the usefulness of results problematic. Only five evaluation studies clearly connected data collection, analyses, and recommendations; of them, one is a qualitative study of a small sample of universities and departments (Richter 1984), one is a historical assessment of a university-based research corporation (Blumenthal, Epstein, and Maxwell 1986), one is a macrosocietal critique of business-university liaisons (Slaughter n.d.), one is a survey of the participants in the National Science Foundation Engineering Research Centers (U.S. General Accounting Office 1988), and one is a national survey of biotechnology faculty (Blumenthal et al. 1986).

The majority of the writings on industry-university relationships are "position papers" based on personal experiences or second- and third-hand data and distinctly ideological in focus. Even some of the research-based literature (e.g., Johnston and Edwards 1987; Public Policy Center 1986) and findings based on substantial personal experience at a specific campus (e.g., Bok 1982) are strongly influenced by beliefs about the nature of institutions of higher education and their role in economic development (Teich 1982, p. 104).

Underlying the ideological positions are significant political

The most striking impact of these ideological and political agendas is the lack of interest in evaluating the effectiveness of industry-university research relationships.

---

agendas for corporations, academic institutions, and state and federal governments. Many of the strongest advocates of increased federal and state government investment in business-university liaisons, for example, are chief executive officers of the organizations most likely to benefit from such an investment (Slaughter n.d.). The most striking impact of these ideological and political agendas is the lack of interest in evaluating the effectiveness of industry-university research relationships and of asking whether the investment is worth the cost to university, corporate, and governmental investors.

A continuum of ideological positions regarding industry-university liaisons ranges from strong advocacy to advocacy with recognition of management and legal concerns to caution with little belief in positive benefits to opposition. The advocates outnumber the opponents; few are in between the two extremes.

The Advocates
The advocates of industry-university liaisons consist of three sources: government; academe; and a broad coalition that includes industry, nonprofit organizations, and national associations.

Government
In the past decade, federal (National Research Council 1985a, 1985b, 1985c, 1985d; National Science Board 1986; National Science Foundation 1982b) and state (Chmura, Henton, and Melville 1988; Lynton and Elman 1987; Public Policy Center 1986) governments have advocated the use of alliances between business and higher education to promote economic growth:

> *More extensive and closer relations between industry and academe are potentially beneficial to all parties. For universities, they offer exposure to marketplace needs, diversification of funding sources, and availability of modern instrumentation, each of which can improve the soundness and broaden the scope of research. Industry benefits when its relations with academe help sustain and augment the flow of graduates and the scientific base supporting commercial technology. These results contribute to the economy and security of the United States* (National Academy of Sciences 1983, p. 10).

The increase in state investment to promote technology transfer from university to industry has been especially visible (Feller 1986, 1988; National Academy of Engineering 1988; Skocpol 1985; Slaughter n.d.; U.S. Office of Technology Assessment 1984), and the principal focus has been on high-technology disciplines, particularly in science and engineering (National Research Council 1985b; Office of Science and Technology Policy 1986). Indeed, the state focus has been so exclusively on promoting economic development through high technology that its involvement can be interpreted as an attempt to "order the claims, interest, and energies of the higher education policy formation process" (Slaughter n.d.).

Academe

The academic advocates consist of those who believe the mission of their institutions includes a strong role in economic development, those who criticize current academic practices, and those who claim that academic institutions must adjust to meet their competitors who form liaisons with industry. Community college leaders and administrators from some regional comprehensive colleges and universities are among the first group, claiming that the mission of their institutions is directly tied to the local and regional economy (Day 1985; Hurwitz 1982; Lynton and Elman 1987; McMullen 1984; Parnell 1986; Parnell and Yarrington 1982; Public Policy Center 1986). The second group advocates increased attention by academic institutions to societal needs (Cross 1981; Lynton 1981; Schuh 1986). Recommendations include increased flexibility in the provision and adaptation of instruction, including incorporation of industrial staff into curricular decision making (Lynton 1981, p. 14). Also included are calls for dramatic changes in faculty attitudes to respond to industrial needs (Azaroff 1982, p. 33) and for colleges and universities to play a direct role in technology transfer (Lynton and Elman 1987, pp. 1–2).

The final group advocates forming liaisons with industry to maintain their competitive status with various constituencies. For these advocates, relationships with industry are crucial to obtain the necessary funds and visibility to attract and keep talented faculty and students. Also important for public institutions is demonstrating responsiveness to state initiatives for technology transfer, which may affect funding for colleges and universities (Feller 1988).

These arguments, whether aimed at instruction or technology

transfer, are based on the image of academic institutions as active participants in society. This perspective is directly opposed to the concept of colleges and universities as ivory towers removed from external pressures. To these critics, the image of an ivory tower is nonproductive and, in reality, a myth:

> *Any university that insisted on absolute academic freedom, without any limitations or restrictions, would be obligated to decline most governmental, philanthropic, and corporate funding* (Hutt 1983, p. 109).

Industry, nonprofit organizations, and associations

Many industrial leaders are advocates of increased ties with academe (Aerospace Industries 1983; Battenburg 1980; Branscomb 1984; David 1982; Lyon 1982; Stauffer 1979). For some corporate leaders, the emphasis is on enhancing competitiveness and profit by obtaining public subsidies for industrial research and development (Slaughter n.d.). Other industrialists, however, look beyond their own companies and argue that industry-university partnerships enhance the good of society. Some industrialists have supported corporate funding of basic research in addition to more narrowly targeted applied research and product development (Lyon 1982). Others have recognized the importance of the university as a producer of the graduates who form the technical work force for corporate research (David 1982).

As explored in later sections, these distinct industrial objectives—increased competitiveness or profit on the one hand and support for basic research and training of students on the other—are supported by quite different funding mechanisms. For example, narrowly defined research agreements to support applied research may be developed to enhance competitiveness, whereas less restrictive corporate donations might attempt to enhance the more traditional academic goals of basic research and training students. It is not at all clear whether these objectives and their corresponding funding mechanisms are compatible with a variety of university and even corporate goals.

Several national associations, nonprofit research organizations, and other interested parties also have advocated stronger links between business and higher education (Bach and Thornton 1983; Public Policy Center 1986; Smith 1986; Stauffer 1986; Theede 1985). As one example, in 1978 the American Council on Education formed the Business–Higher Education

Forum to promote industry-university cooperation (Dickson 1984, p. 87).

The principal focus of advocates from industry and nonprofit organizations also has been to ensure the vitality of the economy (Hurwitz 1982; Varrin and Kukich 1985, p. 388). With few exceptions (e.g., Public Policy Center 1986), the positions espoused by this group of advocates are not based on research results.

The Opponents

One group of opponents to industry-university liaisons believes that the university has contributed significantly to society because it has remained (more or less) removed from the pressures of the marketplace (Buchbinder and Newson 1985; Dickson 1984; Noble and Pfund 1980). From this perspective, external pressures that reduce university autonomy harm society:

> *When the university and industry become partners, the entire society is endangered, for the demise of the university as an independent institution will lead to the crippling of the tradition of an independent university* (Kenney 1986, p. 246).

For these opponents, the missions of academic institutions and industry are fundamentally in opposition; formal mechanisms to form alliances cannot alter this conflict:

> *Put quite simply, the proper functions of university research are inconsistent with the profit motives of the private investor and a mere "code of etiquette" for the university will not suffice. No set of procedural safeguards could eradicate the basic substantive inconsistency* (Caldert 1983, pp. 30–31).

These opponents of industry-university liaisons have elaborated potential areas of conflict, ranging from academic freedom to faculty behavior (discussed in subsequent sections). As with the advocates, little data exist to support or contradict these concerns.

A second group of opponents to business-university research liaisons questions the effectiveness of such relationships for economic development. The principal argument for this group is that universities are not efficient or effective direct contributors to economic growth (Blumenthal, Epstein, and Maxwell 1986; Feller 1986, 1988; Nelson 1986; Williams 1986). In addition, the economic return of these liaisons for the university itself is questionable (Blumenthal, Epstein, and Maxwell 1986).

The Moderates

The lack of empirical information, which tends to moderate views by supporting or rejecting (or at least illuminating) competing hypotheses, is partly responsible for the limited number of commentators taking less ideological positions about industry-university relationships. In this group, statements about the ties between business and higher education emphasize the need for careful assessment (what might be gained and lost) and for reasonable expectations (Aslanian and Brickell 1981, pp. 18–19; Rosenzweig and Turlington 1982). Perhaps most significant, the moderates recognize the effect of ideology on how industry-university relationships are judged:

> In large part, how one assesses the impact [of industry-university relationships] depends on how one perceives the nature of the university in general. It may well be unrealistic to assume that the university could be, or should be, "impartial" or a repository of neutral competence. Biases find their way into academic work, although the imprint of bias is not always obvious. Any academic inquiry, including scientific and technical research, involves a multitude of choices among competing interests, methodologies, and viewpoints (Ashford 1983, pp. 19–20).

Industry, institutions of higher education, and their "silent" partners, state and federal governments, are motivated to cooperate for a variety of reasons. These motivating factors vary substantially between government and industry on the one hand and academe on the other. Substantial variation in the motivations for collaboration also exist within each constituency, although in each case a single motivation dominates.

Government

The principal motivation of the federal government in promoting alliances between business and higher education is to increase the competitiveness of American industry and to restore the United States to a dominant (or at least equal) position in technologically oriented disciplines (Geiger 1988; National Science Board 1986; National Science Foundation 1982b). In broad terms, the federal government seeks to make "this considerable public investment in research more available for the development of useful products and processes and eventual commercialization" (National Science Foundation 1982b, p. 17).

In advocating industry-university liaisons, the focus of federal policy is to resolve the trade imbalance, increase productivity, ensure that university research activities meet the needs of industry, increase the transition from basic research to product development, and establish a coherent national research and development plan (Feller 1988; Gavert 1983; National Academy of Engineering 1983; Schmitt 1986). Preferred vehicles for promoting industry-university collaboration are legislation (e.g., change in patent laws) and targeted programs, such as the National Science Foundation's Engineering Research Centers (Association of American Universities 1986; Haddad 1986; Schmitt 1986).

State governments also desire to enhance their economic position, although sometimes at the expense of other states. Some state economic development plans, for example, seek to attract existing industry from other regions (Dowling 1987; Public Policy Center 1986). In this context, state and federal perspectives may clash. When one state "wins" and another "loses," the two states have contrasting views about the outcome; the federal view is that existing resources have been redistributed but the overall economic capacity of the nation has not improved. For this reason, federal programs are more likely to en-

The primary motivation for industry to form partnerships with institutions of higher education is to fulfill requirements for human capital.

courage states to build new industries rather than to attract corporations from neighboring states.

Many state governments also include the creation of new companies as a goal of economic development (Dowling 1987, p. 261). Industry-university partnerships are viewed as mechanisms to create new high-technology industries and, increase the rate of technology transfer, which may create new jobs, develop new products, and prepare trained personnel for the workplace (Association of American Universities 1986; Dowling 1987).

Industry

Spurred by the profit motive, industries form liaisons with academic institutions to improve their competitive position (Association of American Universities 1986; National Science Foundation 1982b; Praeger and Omenn 1980). Although exceptions exist, most corporations contribute to universities in expectation of a short- or long-term economic benefit (Broce 1986). For industry, the potential benefits from collaborating with academic institutions focus on human capital, resources, innovation and product development, and public reputation.

Human capital

The primary motivation for industry to form partnerships with institutions of higher education is to fulfill requirements for human capital. For industry-university liaisons, considerations involving human capital include access to undergraduate and graduate students who may become future employees, access to faculty who are experts in relevant technical fields, and provision of continuing education for professionals (Baldwin and Green 1984–85; Branscomb 1984; Business–Higher Education Forum 1984; David 1982; Geiger 1988; Houle 1980; National Science Foundation 1982b; Peters and Fusfeld 1983; Praeger and Omenn 1980; Smith 1988; Stark, Lowther, and Hagerty 1986).

For industry, the development of human capital is a relatively long-term goal, and it differs from relationships that focus on product development and profit, described later.

Resources

The increasing complexity of research and development has made it difficult for a single corporation to develop a self-sufficient research capacity (National Science Foundation

1982b, p. 16). Gaining access to university research facilities and faculty is an economical solution for many companies:

> It is becoming increasingly difficult for any one industry laboratory to fully encompass the requisite expertise. A partial remedy for this situation is to seek out the pertinent skills wherever they may be found in the nation's universities (Branscomb 1984, p. 46).

Using colleges to provide additional technical training for personnel may also be more economical than expanding in-house training facilities (Boyle 1983).

Innovation and product development

Industry is strongly motivated to work with colleges and universities to improve the transfer of basic research to application in the marketplace (Levin, Cohen, and Mowery 1985; Matthews and Norgaard 1984; National Science Foundation 1982b; Nelson 1982; Peters and Fusfeld 1983), which includes providing industry with a "window of opportunity" through access to research results before their general release. It also emphasizes applied research (Swanson 1986, p. 28). Few industrial leaders expect liaisons with colleges and universities to result directly in product development, however (U.S. General Accounting Office 1988).

Reputation

Corporations desire to enhance their public reputations. By making contributions to colleges and universities to assist in the rebirth of the national economy, corporations can enhance their reputations (Branscomb 1984; National Science Foundation 1982b; Peters and Fusfeld 1983).

Academe

In considering liaisons with industry, academic institutions are motivated by considerations about resources, faculty and students, prestige, and public relations.

Resources

In a steady-state or perhaps declining (in real terms) financial base (Bok 1982; Boyer 1987; Business–Higher Education Forum 1984; Hines 1987), including a leveling of federal research funds (National Science Foundation 1982b, 1984a,

1985d), many colleges and universities are confronted with decaying physical plants and facilities; decreased ability to compete for students, faculty, and research funding; and deteriorating quality of academic programs (Branscomb 1984; Keller 1983; Mai 1984). Meanwhile, the costs of university activities, especially basic research, continue to climb:

> *The fundamental problem is that basic research has become such a large-scale and expensive activity as to constitute a heavy drain on federal budgets, and an intolerable financial burden on the American university. Basically, the problem is money* (Muller 1982, p. 25).

In this fiscal climate, institutions of higher education have sought additional sources of revenue, including funding from industry. From the academic perspective, the principal motivation for forming "new alliances" with industrial partners is financial need (Association of American Universities 1986; Branscomb 1984; Carley 1988; Dimancescu and Botkin 1986; Geiger 1988; Green 1985; Matthews and Norgaard 1984; National Science Foundation 1982b; Noble and Pfund 1980; Peters and Fusfeld 1983; Reams 1986).

The source of external funding also has become an issue in academic administration. Although some observers claim that federally funded research is less restrictive in focus than research funded by industry (e.g., Caldert 1983, p. 27), others argue that federal research funds increasingly are accompanied by extensive regulation, which has reduced the autonomy of academic scientists (Branscomb 1984; Feller 1988; Peters and Fusfeld 1983; Praeger and Omenn 1980; Rosenzweig and Turlington 1982). From this perspective, increased funding from alternative sources, such as industry, enhances faculty independence (Rosenzweig and Turlington 1982).

Faculty and students

As labor-intensive entities, academic institutions place great value on faculty and students. Colleges and universities may view partnerships with industry as a means to gain access to needed part-time faculty (Matthews and Norgaard 1984). These partnerships may also assist in attracting and retaining new full-time faculty by providing access to state-of-the-art facilities and by enhancing salaries (Bach and Thornton 1983; Feller 1988; Kenney 1986). Partnerships between business and higher education may also help attract students by appearing to increase opportunities for job placement (Branscomb 1984; Carley 1988; Feller 1988; National Science Foundation 1982b; Peters and Fusfeld 1983).

Prestige
The aspiration to "move up the prestige ladder" is strong in all types of academic institutions (Carley 1988), and the ability to attract externally funded research has become a benchmark for measuring progress on the ladder (Bowen and Schuster 1986, p. 150). In this context, colleges and universities form partnerships with industry to enhance the size and visibility of their research operations.

Public relations
Finally, responding (or at least appearing to respond) to social needs makes academic institutions appear more accountable. By forming partnerships with industry to revitalize the economy, colleges and universities can enhance their public image (Feller 1988; Geiger 1988; Knorr-Cetina 1981, p. 76).

Summary
The growth of alliances between business and higher education reflects the perception by government, industry, and academe that a significant *overlap* of interests exists. Academic institutions, for example, require additional resources. Industry is willing to provide resources in exchange for access to students, faculty, and resources. Only at the most general level (e.g., desire for an improved economy), however, can academe and industry be said to have *identical* interests; in most cases, institutions of higher education participate in alliances for reasons different from those of their industrial counterparts.

TYPES OF INDUSTRY-UNIVERSITY LIAISONS

The most visible alliances between business and higher education are research agreements between large corporations and prominent academic institutions (e.g., Hoechst and Harvard University, Monsanto and Washington University, Exxon and Massachusetts Institute of Technology). These arrangements account, however, for only a small portion of all relationships between academic institutions and industry, many of which do not have economic development as a theme (National Science Board 1986; Ping 1981). This section examines the full array of business–higher education liaisons, including the types of participants, the kinds of disciplines in which relationships occur, and alternative typologies for classifying such alliances.

The Participants

Participants in alliances between business and higher education can include industry, colleges and universities and their faculty, government laboratories, nonprofit research centers, and venture capital firms (National Research Council 1985c). The three principal groups of participants—industry, academic institutions, and faculty—are discussed in the following paragraphs.

Industry

From an industrial perspective, liaisons with industrial academic institutions can be grouped into formal collaborative research agreements and other types of liaisons.

Formal collaborative research agreements. Most formal collaborative research agreements between industry and academe are funded by major corporations with substantial internal research and development capacity (Feller 1988; Fusfeld and Haklisch 1987; Link and Tassey 1987; Logan and Stampen 1985; National Science Board 1987; National Science Foundation 1982b). Although relatively small overall (about 6 percent of the total), industrial funding for academic research represents a substantial proportion of research income for some institutions and disciplines (Ashford 1983, pp. 16–17; National Science Board 1985, 1987). Small- and medium-sized companies are conspicuously absent in large-scale research-oriented relationships with universities.

For large corporations, liaisons with universities are supplemental to in-house research rather than replacements for it. Large corporations without the internal capacity for research are less likely to participate in research agreements with universi-

Small- and medium-sized companies are conspicuously absent in large-scale research-oriented relationships with universities.

ties or, if they do participate, to take advantage of research results (Fusfeld and Haklisch 1987; Link and Tassey 1987).

Product focus is also related to the likelihood of a corporation's working collaboratively with universities on research projects. The most frequent corporate participants in industry-university research relationships represent six product types: chemicals, electronics, food, manufacturing, petroleum, and pharmaceuticals (National Science Foundation 1982b, p. 20). Companies producing and selling these types of products place greater emphasis on research and innovation than companies centering primarily on marketing and sales (Lawrence and Lorsch 1967, pp. 138–41).

Biotechnology has been an especially important discipline in the formation of business-university liaisons (Kenney 1986). The characteristics of this discipline that have encouraged research relationships with industry include the small pool of research scientists (in academe and industry), the commercial applicability of biotechnology research results across a variety of types of industry, changes in patent laws that permit more open participation by universities and their faculty, and the relatively short research–product development cycle (Williams 1986).

Other factors affecting the likelihood of a corporation's entering into a research agreement with a university include sophistication of the research program, geographic proximity, fiscal strength, quality of leadership, and past history of relationships with an academic institution (Broce 1986; Geiger 1988; National Science Board 1987; National Science Foundation 1982b; Praeger and Omenn 1980).

Other types of liaisons. In addition to the highly visible research agreements between major corporations and universities, many companies have other types of relationships with academic institutions; they include research agreements with individual faculty, donations and contributions, and education and training. When these additional relationships are taken into account, total corporate support for higher education is considerably greater than the level indicated by contributions for research and development (National Science Foundation 1982b, p. 10).

Many companies have consulting agreements with individual faculty, often focused on research (David 1982; Low 1983; National Science Foundation 1982b). Contract research or purchase agreements are also common forms of liaison, much more so than the multimillion dollar collaborative research agreements (David 1982; Low 1983; National Science Foundation 1982b; Smith 1988).

Large and small companies also make donations and contributions to a variety of academic institutions: donations to general operating funds, usually in the form of matching gifts, assistance in upgrading facilities, loans of equipment and discounts for equipment purchase, hiring students and faculty for summer work, funds to supplement faculty salaries, and access to company facilities (Business–Higher Education Forum 1984; David 1982; Harris 1988; National Academy of Sciences 1983; National Science Foundation 1982b; Peters and Fusfeld 1983).

Finally, some companies make corporate staff available for part-time instruction, develop and fund scholarships, provide on-the-job training for students, and conduct continuing education and retraining programs (Business–Higher Education Forum 1984; Eurich 1985; National Academy of Sciences 1983; National Science Foundation 1982b; Smith 1988).

Academic institutions

In the broad definition of "liaison," participating academic institutions range from major research universities to comprehensive colleges and universities to two-year colleges and proprietary institutions. Like industry, academe is characterized by diversity, not homogeneity (Clark 1987).

Academic institutions also vary by their capacity to play a leadership role in specific disciplines and activities. Institutions whose faculty are on the frontier of knowledge have the capacity to lead industry to new discoveries. Other institutions are better able to respond to existing needs, assisting industry through technical assistance, continuing education, and the like. The position of a college or university on this leadership-responsiveness continuum, which may vary by discipline, is related to its likely impact on regional economic development, continuing professional education, and so on.

Research universities. The most visible academic participants in alliances between business and higher education are research universities. These institutions receive the majority of total research funds, corporate research funds, and corporate philanthropic contributions. Between 1970 and 1980, the top 10 research universities (out of approximately 3,000 four-year institutions) received 20 percent of all research and development funds, the top 20 received between 40 percent and 50 percent, and the top 100 received 84 percent (Drew 1985, pp. 64–65; National Science Board 1985, pp. 92–109; National Science Foundation 1982b, pp. 6–11). Similarly, doctorate-granting universities receive by far the largest percentage (70 percent) of voluntary support from corporations (Council for Financial Aid 1988, p. 7).

Research universities also house the majority of formal research relationships with industry; a 1982 study found that the 463 industry-university research relationships were located in only 39 universities (Peters and Fusfeld 1983). And by locating most of its Engineering Research Centers in major universities, the National Science Foundation has reinforced this trend (Haddad 1986, p. 132). Unlike regionally oriented four-year institutions, elite research universities have a national agenda (Feller 1988, pp. 21–22; Friedman and Friedman 1985), a focus that can conflict with the interest of state governments in promoting local and regional economic development (Public Policy Center 1986).

Research universities also are not homogeneous with respect to capability in different disciplines, availability of funds, and the like. Nor do research universities share a common view about their role in technology transfer (Association of American Universities 1986, p. 12). Finally, differences in the willingness and ability to form research alliances with industry exist between public and private institutions. For example, although public and private universities have been willing to enter into long-term industry-university research agreements in biotechnology, all but two of these relationships involve private universities (Kenney 1986, p. 57), reflecting the greater ability of private institutions, on average, in basic sciences.

These findings suggest that the term "research university" does not connote homogeneity on many dimensions related to forming liaisons with industry. Research agreements involving, for example, Stanford University or the Massachusetts Institute of Technology, may not be generalizable to other academic institutions.

Other four-year institutions. Most four-year colleges and universities do not emphasize research, especially expensive basic research. Some commentators claim that doctorate-granting and comprehensive colleges and universities (see Carnegie Commission 1976, e.g.) can play a strong role in regional economic development (Feller 1988; Friedman and Friedman 1985; Public Policy Center 1986; Sheppard 1986). Yet little attention has been paid to existing and potential liaisons between industry and this type of four-year institution (Logan and Stampen 1985). The limited existing evidence suggests that comprehensive colleges and universities focus attention on smaller, local companies, focus on regional and local economic and educational needs, and are less likely to be concerned about potential negative results from partnerships with industry:

> The predominating attitude [at comprehensive institutions] seems to be that industry is a constituency like any other having a legitimate claim on university services. Also, like other constituencies, industry offers resources that can be used to improve educational programs (Logan and Stampen 1985, p. 29).

As for research universities, comprehensive colleges and doctorate-granting institutions do not share a common view of relations with industry. In some institutions, many new faculty are recent graduates of leading research institutions and desire to carry out basic research (Drew 1985, p. 67), adding impetus to the aspiration to move up the prestige ladder. Comprehensives colleges and universities with such faculty may see themselves as potential partners in large-scale research agreements with industry; smaller relationships emphasizing local technology transfer may not be as appealing to these institutions and their faculty.

Two-year colleges and proprietary institutions. Often overlooked are the substantial ties between industry and community and junior colleges and proprietary institutions. Community colleges have had and continue to play a major role in local and regional economies (American Association of Community and Junior Colleges 1984; Boyle 1983; Ellison 1983; Parnell 1986; Parnell and Yarrington 1982; Rinehart 1982; Samuels 1985). Several states officially recognize the usefulness of two-year institutions in promoting economic development, including California (Duscha 1984), Illinois (Burger 1984), and Virginia (McMullen 1984).

Most of these institutions are not reluctant to form liaisons with industry, especially for personnel development and training (Day 1985). The large majority have developed the following types of relationships with industry: using business/labor/industry councils in academic decision making, hiring a person to act as liaison with local industry, offering employee training programs, providing on-site training programs, and working actively with local and regional economic development offices. A much smaller percentage offer technical assistance and retraining programs (Day 1985, pp. 13–20, 31).

Faculty

Like their institutions, faculty involved in industrially supported ventures are not a homogeneous or representative group. Industry tends to work with faculty familiar with its operations (Branscomb 1984, p. 45), which limits the potential pool of faculty participants. Because industrial support for academic research is concentrated in a few fields, faculty involved in industrially funded research tend to represent a handful of disciplines. Faculty entrepreneurial activity, especially the formation of faculty-owned companies, also seems to cluster in a few disciplines, especially biotechnology, engineering, and computer science (Kenney 1986; Peters and Fusfeld 1983). Faculty within a discipline also vary significantly in their involvement with industry (Blumenthal et al. 1986, p. 1362). Finally, faculty receiving substantial research support from industry also seem to have significant support from federal sources (Richter 1984, p. 27).

Each descriptor indicates that industry-university relationships rely on relatively few faculty in a specific set of disciplines. This concentration may have significant implications for faculty workloads and behavior.

The Disciplines

Industry has concentrated its funding of academic research in relatively few fields, emphasizing technical areas of particular importance to the corporate sponsor (Branscomb 1984, p. 44). These disciplines include engineering, computer science, medicine, agriculture, chemistry, and, more recently, biotechnology (Blumenthal et al. 1986; Kenney 1986; National Science Board 1987; Nelson 1986; Peters and Fusfeld 1983; Wofsy 1986). Within engineering, particular attention has been paid to electrical and mechanical engineering and to newer fields, such as manufacturing engineering, materials engineering, and robotics (Holmstrom and Petrovich 1985).

The little evidence that exists suggests that faculty in chemistry and engineering receive most of the industrial funds for academic research, followed by faculty in fields related to biotechnology (Blumenthal et al. 1986; National Science Board 1987). If consulting arrangements and other types of industry-university alliances are included, faculty in business, management, economics, and related fields also have substantial contact with industry.

The acceptability of liaisons with industry also varies considerably by discipline. Faculty and administrators in applied professional fields, such as engineering, traditionally have found liaisons with industry more consistent with perceived academic missions than their counterparts in liberal arts (Hambrick and Swanson 1979, p. 130). Although the recent emphasis on industry-university collaboration has been on high technology (Johnson 1984), fields like chemical engineering have a much longer tradition of cooperation with industry.

The procedure for initiating research agreements with industry also varies by discipline. For most fields, university personnel initiate contact with industry (Johnson and Tornatzky 1984); in microelectronics, however, the reverse is true (Larsen and Wigand 1987, p. 588).

Industrial investment in particular academic disciplines can be substantial (Ashford 1983, pp. 16–17). In biotechnology, for example, nearly half of all companies have some type of arrangement with universities, and these companies account for between 16 and 24 percent of all university funding for biotechnology (Blumenthal et al. 1986). In some institutions, this percentage is substantially higher (Kenney 1986; Richter 1984).

These findings suggest that the lessons learned from industry-university alliances in particular disciplines may not apply to other fields. In addition, the impact of industry-university relationships on faculty and student behavior is likely to be much stronger in some fields than in others.

Typologies of Industry-University Liaisons
Several typologies describing relationships between business and higher education have been developed (see, e.g., Haller 1984; Peters and Fusfeld 1983; Zinser 1982).[1] Most select a

1. For lists of specific industry-university relationships refer especially to Association of American Universities (1986), Johnson (1984), National Science Foundation (1982b), Peters and Fusfeld (1983), and Public Policy Center (1986).

particular perspective, such as the contractual mechanism, and classify a set of industry-university alliances accordingly. These approaches have provided little institutional-level information, which has limited their utility for academic administrators (Feller 1988, p. 4).

As elaborated below, industry-university liaisons can be categorized by academic function, industrial function, economic development activity, organizational location, intimacy of working relationship, and collaborative mechanism.

Academic function

From the academic perspective, industry-university partnerships can be classified into research related, instruction related, administration related, and service related.

Research-related liaisons. The majority of industrial funds given to academic institutions focus on research (National Science Board 1986; Ping 1981). Industry-university research relationships range from consulting arrangements with individual faculty to large-scale, long-term research contracts between corporations and research universities.

Many industry-university research relationships focus on technology transfer (Baldwin and Green 1984–85; Johnson 1984; Larsen and Wigand 1987)—transfer of knowledge from university faculty to industrial staff, upgraded training of industrial scientists, creation of spinoff companies, and provision of technical assistance (Baldwin and Green 1984–85; Larsen and Wigand 1987).

The focus of industrially funded academic research is typically on applied rather than on basic research (Blumenthal et al. 1986; Branscomb 1984; Hutt 1983; National Science Foundation 1982b; Peters and Fusfeld 1983; Tatel and Guthrie 1983; Wofsy 1986). As discussed in later sections, the concentration of substantial industrial funds in a few fields with a focus on applied research has potential consequences for academic research, teaching, and service-related activities.

Instruction-related liaisons. Industry is much less likely to contribute funds directly for traditional academic instructional activities (National Science Board 1986; Ping 1981). When funds are made available, the focus is usually on graduate education, not undergraduate instruction (Fairweather n.d.). A few corporations have contributed part-time faculty to colleges and universities, especially in fields with shortages of faculty (Fair-weather n.d.). Others have funded graduate assistantships as part of research arrangements (Praeger and Omenn 1980), al-though technicians may be used in place of graduate students in some industry-university partnerships (Fairweather n.d.).

Industrial participation in continuing professional education is more apparent. The need for upgraded training in technical fields has made continuing education a natural "bridge" be-tween business and higher education (Brooks 1984; Foster 1986; Moser 1986; National Research Council 1985a; Nowlen and Stern 1981). Despite the interest of industry, many colleges continue to emphasize formal degree programs in continuing studies (Stark, Lowther, and Hagerty 1986; Walker and Low-enthal 1981) or fail to incorporate continuing education into the academic mainstream (National Research Council 1985a).

As a consequence, industry increasingly plays a direct role in continuing education. At least 18 corporations now offer ac-credited degree programs (Chmura, Henton, and Melville 1987; Eurich 1985). The majority of continuing education faculty in engineering are from industry, not academe (National Research Council 1985a, p. 51). And industry has increased the use of alternative suppliers of continuing education, including national associations, proprietary schools, and individual consultants (Houle 1980, pp. 167–99).

The majority of continuing education faculty in engineering are from industry, not academe.

Administration-related liaisons. Although seldom considered in the literature, industrial leaders play considerable roles in the administration of academic institutions. Usually at an individual level, corporate directors frequently serve on boards of trustees, assisting universities to make difficult decisions about the allo-cation of resources. Heads of companies also direct many uni-versity fundraising activities, especially national campaigns (Harris 1988). Industrial managers and scientists also serve on academic advisory boards, advising department heads and faculty.

Service-related liaisons. Industry-university alliances incorpo-rate service-related activities in two ways. The first concerns the development of human capital (Johnson 1984). In addition to continuing professional education activities, some industrial partnerships with community colleges address job training and retraining (Burger 1984; Derber 1987; Duscha 1984; Ellison

1983; Samuels 1985), and a few four-year institutions also address job training and retraining (Charner and Rolzinski 1987).

Businesses also form liaisons with higher education to develop scientists and engineers for the future (Johnson 1984). A program to unite industry, colleges, and high schools in encouraging students to major in teacher education of mathematics and science is an example of this type of relationship (Clark 1984).

Finally, some collaborative arrangements focus on remediation and basic skills (Foster 1986; Winkler 1982). Activities to increase adult literacy also come under this category.

A second service orientation concerns economic benefits. In contrast to the activities related more to human capital, which are indirectly related to economic development, some partnerships aim directly to increase employment, generate start-up companies, and stimulate economic expansion (Fox 1985). The Ben Franklin Partnership in Pennsylvania, for example, defines success in terms of increased opportunities for employment (Corporation for Penn State 1986).

Industrial function

From the industrial perspective, relationships with academic institutions can be classified into two types: (1) agreements related directly or indirectly to business concerns and (2) philanthropic contributions (Alexander 1988, p. 13). Virtually any collaborative mechanism can fit into either type, depending on the intent of the arrangement.

Economic development

Industry-university liaisons can be classified according to economic development activity. In this scheme, categories include human resource development, economic research and analysis, enhancing the economic capacity of regional organizations, technical assistance, advanced research, technology transfer, and developing new businesses (Public Policy Center 1986, p. 11).

Organizational location

Relationships between business and higher education can be classified according to placement in the academic partner. Organizational distinctions are crucial because the location of the alliance can affect faculty and administrative behavior (Ikenberry and Friedman 1972; Teich 1982). Placement of a collaborative agreement in an academic department, on the one extreme, reinforces the traditional academic reward structure and faculty behavior. Establishing organized research units independent from traditional academic structures, however, may reinforce interdisciplinary research goals while deemphasizing instructional and advising roles for faculty (Teich 1982, p. 96).

The location of industry-university partnerships can be classified into three levels: individual, intrainstitutional, and institutional.

Individual arrangements. Although alliances between business and higher education often are institutional arrangements, the most typical form—consulting—is an arrangement between a company and a faculty member (Battenburg 1980; Low 1983). Grants and contracts also can be used to form relations between individual faculty and a corporation. Faculty-initiated businesses and other individual entrepreneurial activities are also conducted at the individual level.

Intrainstitutional locations. Industry-university relationships also exist at the departmental level, tying a group of faculty and relevant administrators with a company or companies. Several biotechnology agreements, for example, create ties between entire departments and a corporation (Kenney 1986).

Some affiliations between academe and industry sometimes are housed in interdisciplinary research organizations or organized research units (ORUs) (Friedman and Freidman 1984). These innovative arrangements might permit universities to incorporate and support activities that would be resisted in traditional departments:

> When universities set up ORUs, they are choosing to pursue activities for which departments, for one reason or another, are deemed to be inappropriate. In this sense, ORUs represent a primary means by which universities can adapt to changes in their environments (Teich 1982, p. 99).

Interdisciplinary research units vary considerably in their source of financial support. The continuum ranges from complete dependence on university funds to complete dependence on external funds (Geiger 1986). Location on this continuum has implications for the behavior of faculty, administrators, and students. For example, an ORU whose faculty depend completely on external funds for research, summer stipends, and graduate assistantships may spend substantially more time pursuing funds than faculty in a unit where such activities are supported with funds from the university.

Institutional level. Gifts and donations of equipment are examples of industry-university affiliations at the institutional level. Such arrangements are usually philanthropic rather than business-related contributions (Alexander 1988).

Finally, some industry-university relationships involve consortia, which may involve a single university with several industrial partners or a single corporate participant working with several universities (Johnson 1984; Low 1983; Zinser 1982).

Intimacy of working relationship

Agreements between industry and academic institutions can be classified by the degree to which goals and operations are shared. More distant relationships include corporate contributions and procurements or purchases. Agreements that require closer working relationships include formal links or networks and exchange programs (personnel and technology transfer). The closest working relationships involve cooperative alliances, such as research agreements involving shared daily activities between industrial staff and faculty, and joint ventures (Zinser 1982).

The relationship between the goals and functions of any industry-university liaison and the goals and missions of both academic and corporate partners has important consequences for assessing the impact of these liaisons on participants. Research agreements that permit faculty to follow their own research agendas, for example, differ dramatically in their continuity with academic practices from agreements that dictate research agendas. (These issues are discussed more fully in subsequent sections.)

Collaborative mechanism

Industry-university relationships can be classified according to the mechanism used to achieve collaboration: donations and contributions, research agreements, technology transfer, education and training, and professional development. These categories are not mutually exclusive; personnel exchange programs, for example, may contribute to professional development *and* to technology transfer.

In these collaborative mechanisms, little emphasis is given to the manufacturing, production, and distribution cycles of innovation, areas evidently accepted as within the industrial domain.

Donations and contributions. Voluntary support for postsecondary institutions by corporations is a substantial source of revenue for many colleges and universities: Voluntary corporate support almost matches that from alumni (21.4 percent versus 27.6 percent) and exceeds that from foundations (17.8 percent). From 1981 to 1987, voluntary corporate support for academic programs increased as rapidly as that from alumni, which was highest (43.3 percent versus 45.5 percent), far exceeding the increase in support from foundations (16 percent) (Council for Financial Aid 1988, p. 3).

Corporate philanthropic support for academic institutions takes various forms. At the institutional level, unrestricted gifts and matching gifts are common forms of contribution (Eurich 1985; Harris 1988; Kenney 1986; National Academy of Sciences 1983; National Science Foundation 1982b; Praeger and Omenn 1980). Contributions with a generic purpose also are common; they include funds for capital expenditures and improvement of facilities, donations of equipment and discounts on purchases, endowed professorships, and unrestricted funds for use in a chosen field or activity (e.g., research) (Eurich 1985; National Academy of Sciences 1983; National Science Foundation 1982b; Peters and Fusfeld 1983; Praeger and Omenn 1980).

Corporations also make donations to support students, typically by establishing fellowship or scholarship programs (Business–Higher Education Forum 1984; Kenney 1986; National Science Foundation 1982b; Praeger and Omenn 1980; Smith 1988). They can either be unrestricted or limited to specific types of students or programs.

Research agreements. Consulting agreements with individual faculty are the most common form of industry-university research agreement (Battenburg 1980; Business–Higher Education Forum 1984; David 1982; Foster 1986; Johnson 1984; Kenney 1986; Low 1983; National Science Foundation 1982b; Praeger and Omenn 1980). These agreements can be long term or developed for a specific project.

At the institutional and departmental levels, the variation in types of industry-university research agreements is considerably greater than at the individual faculty level. Typical approaches include grants, contracts, and design participation programs, where a group of students try to solve a problem submitted by a company (Battenburg 1980; David 1982; Foster 1986; Johnson 1984; Low 1983; National Science Foundation 1982b; Praeger and Omenn 1980; Smith 1988). More recent types of research agreements include cooperative research projects, which range from small nonproprietary projects to large proprietary contracts; long-term, large-scale research agreements, which may result in formal partnerships; and research centers and institutes (David 1982; Johnson 1984; Kenney 1986; National Science Foundation 1982b; Praeger and Omenn 1980).

Collaborative research mechanisms can be bilateral, involving single industrial and academic partners (Business–Higher Education Forum 1984; Johnson 1984). Alternatively, a consortium of industrial and/or academic participants can be involved (Battenburg 1980; Business–Higher Education Forum 1984; David 1982; Johnson 1984; Low 1983; National Science Foundation 1982b).

Research agreements also can be classified according to arrangements for responsibility and leadership. Research projects in industry-university agreements can be jointly developed and operated, operated in parallel with industry and university scientists competing to find solutions, or primarily directed by either university faculty or industrial scientists (National Research Council 1985c, pp. 19–20).

Technology transfer. The growth of industry-university alliances is best seen in the rapid expansion of agreements to promote technology transfer. Traditional mechanisms include conferences, colloquia, and symposia; publications, including work jointly authored by faculty and industrial staff; extension programs, particularly in agriculture; and industry advisory councils and research advisory committees (Battenburg 1980; Business–Higher Education Forum 1984; David 1982; Geiger 1988; Johnson 1984; National Research Council 1985c; National Science Board 1987). Industrial affiliate or associate programs, where one or more corporations gain access to faculty research results and university facilities for a fee, also are common (Battenburg 1980; Business–Higher Education Forum 1984; David 1982; Johnson 1984; Kenney 1986; Low 1983; National Science Foundation 1982b; Praeger and Omenn 1980). In addition, research parks are well established as mechanisms for technology transfer (Low 1983, pp. 72–73), although a wider variety of academic institutions recently have attempted to develop research parks (Carley 1988, p. 27).

Innovations in mechanisms for technology transfer recently have expanded dramatically. These innovations include the use of industrial incubators to develop new companies, private patent companies to secure rights for sale, expanded university research offices to monitor and promote licensing of technology to industry, research and development limited partnerships where a university contracts with a particular corporation to develop products from faculty research findings, nonprofit organizations (e.g., Wisconsin Alumni Research Fund, Brown University Research Fund), independent for-profit entities originated by universities (e.g., Michigan Research Corporation), for-profit joint ventures, often including participation by venture capital firms, and wholly owned subsidiaries (e.g., Washington University Technology Associates, Case Western University Technology, Inc.) (Association of American Universities 1986; Bartlett and Siena 1983–84; Johnson 1984; Kenney 1986; Low 1983).

Education and training. In addition to corporate philanthropy, collaborative arrangements to provide education and training have the longest history of industry-university liaisons. Education and training arrangements include cooperative education, continuing professional education, including programs designed specifically for industrial staff, and corporate contracts with community colleges to provide technical training for staff (Business–Higher Education Forum 1984; Eurich 1985; National Research Council 1985c).

Funding of individuals also has received substantial support. Relevant mechanisms include corporate reimbursement for the educational expenses of staff, internships for students, and summer jobs for students (Battenburg 1980; Business–Higher Education Forum 1984; David 1982; Eurich 1985). Finally, a few corporations have supported academic instruction by encouraging staff to work as part-time instructors and by providing salary supplements to assist universities in retaining junior faculty (Business–Higher Education Forum 1984; Eurich 1985; Peters and Fusfeld 1983).

Professional development. Although professional development may be a function of additional education and training, many corporations view the enhancement of personnel as an end in itself (Foster 1986; Praeger and Omenn 1980). The favorite mechanism for promoting professional development is to incorporate personnel exchanges as components of research agreements (Business–Higher Education Forum 1984; Johnson 1984; Low 1983; National Science Foundation 1982b). Additional approaches include support of faculty sabbaticals and provision of summer employment for faculty (Battenburg 1980; Business–Higher Education Forum 1984; David 1982).

OPERATIONAL ISSUES

Despite the seeming "inevitability" of liaisons between industry and academe, fundamental differences remain in motivation, goals, organizational structures, and employees' attitudes and behavior. Resolution of these differences is crucial to establishing any industry-university relationship and making it work. This section discusses the keys to successful implementation of alliances between business and higher education, elaborates important factors in the successful operation of industry-university liaisons, and presents differing views about the role of management in resolving fundamental differences.

Keys to Successful Implementation

To establish liaisons between industry and academe, as many as nine types of potential barriers and/or supporting conditions must be addressed: historical factors, demographic characteristics, overlap of needs, institutional vulnerability, leadership, culture and mission, academic freedom, legal issues, and potential rewards.

Historical factors

Corporations and academic institutions with existing links are more likely to establish additional formal relationships, although little evidence exists to indicate whether or not philanthropic relationships might lead to research partnerships. For any industry-university relationship, previous experience working together promotes mutual understanding of goals and administrative procedures (Branscomb 1984, p. 45). Extensive exchanges of personnel enhance this process. Alumni serving on corporate governing boards and industrialists serving on university governing boards also enhance this transfer of knowledge (Praeger and Omenn 1980, p. 381).

For research-related partnerships, previous involvement in economic development by either partner may also promote mutual understanding and increase the likelihood of successful implementation. For example, universities with previous commitments to and experience in economic development seem better able to carry out technology transfer (Public Policy Center 1986, pp. 44–46). Universities and corporations with previous collaborative experience may also be more realistic in their expectations, making successful implementation more likely (Public Policy Center 1986, p. 7; Rosenzweig and Turlington 1982, p. 52).

The evolution of corporations and academic institutions can

The increasing role of state governments in providing incentives for universities to assist industry in the transfer of technology to their marketplace has made it imperative politically and financially for public universities to seek liaisons with industry.

also impede the implementation of industry-university alliances by creating competition. Collaboration can become difficult as universities create for-profit ventures and become involved in searching for direct applications of research results (Feller 1988, p. 25) and as industry expands into education and training (Eurich 1985).

Demographic characteristics

The demographic characteristics of corporations and academic institutions affect the implementation of alliances. The first characteristic, proximity, is a shared trait. The other traits listed are presented separately for each type of institution.

Proximity. Geographic proximity is important to the formation of industry-university alliances. Proximity is crucial to philanthropic activities (Broce 1986) as well as to research relationships. Many companies invest in universities to benefit their employees by enhancing the quality of local services (National Science Foundation 1982b; Peters and Fusfeld 1983; Praeger and Omenn 1980). The *strategic* location of a college or university, such as proximity to a state capital or to specific companies, is also important. In this instance, proximity is important in fostering interpersonal communication (Public Policy Center 1986).

Industry. For industry, four demographic characteristics are important in establishing liaisons with institutions of higher education: profitability, size, product line, and orientation toward research. Profitability affects the extent to which a company can support external activities (Praeger and Omenn 1980). Regardless of interest, companies in poor financial health find it difficult to support substantial alliances with academic institutions.

Size is also important. For research relationships, larger companies are more likely than smaller ones to work with universities (Feller 1988; Fusfeld and Haklisch 1987; Link and Tassey 1987; Logan and Stampen 1985; National Science Foundation 1982b). Larger companies also have a better understanding of how university research can best benefit the company (Geiger 1988; Praeger and Omenn 1980). For other types of relationships, such as providing summer jobs for students and granting release time for staff to serve as faculty, size is also important; large companies typically have greater slack resources than their smaller counterparts.

Product line is important to the formation of industry-university research relationships. Relatively few types of industry participate in research relationships with universities (e.g., chemicals, engineering, computer science, biotechnology) (National Science Foundation 1982b; Praeger and Omenn 1980). Further, corporations emphasizing research and manufacturing are in greater need of faculty expertise than companies emphasizing sales and marketing (Lawrence and Lorsch 1967).

Finally, firms with strong, sophisticated research and development departments are more likely to form liaisons with academic institutions than their less research-oriented counterparts (Fowler 1984; Geiger 1988). Such firms are more aware of individual faculty research and the potential utility of faculty research to the company. And a substantial research capacity enhances the credibility of a corporation with colleges and universities:

> *Peer collaboration is only possible when the industrial partner has a significant, progressive in-house research capability employing accomplished scientists and engineers with acceptable academic credentials* (Praeger and Omenn 1980, p. 381).

Academic institutions. Whether an institution is a research university, comprehensive college, or community college, type of institution affects the likelihood of forming certain types of alliances (Praeger and Omenn 1980). Research universities are more likely partners for large-scale research relationships, for example, whereas community colleges traditionally have played substantial roles in retraining industrial staff.

Although some authors claim that size of academic institution contributes to establishing liaisons with industry (e.g., Praeger and Omenn 1980), the relationship is unclear. As an example, for research relationships the orientation of the university seems more important than its size. It is more likely that size of the participating department, which is related to its reputation and visibility (Fairweather 1988), is important (Branscomb 1984; Dickson 1984).

Overlap of needs
The initiation of industry-university alliances depends on the strength and immediacy of specific needs and the degree to

which these needs overlap for a given set of industrial and academic institutions (Bok 1982, p. 149). For example, a university requiring substantial financial resources to continue a basic research program might be more amenable to forming a partnership with a corporation that has sufficient resources to invest. In the same context, corporate leaders might collaborate to gain access to advanced knowledge in a field on which their future depends.

Institutional vulnerability
The increasing role of state governments in providing incentives for universities to assist industry in the transfer of technology to their marketplace has made it imperative politically and financially for public universities (and for private institutions receiving substantial state subsidies) to seek liaisons with industry (Slaughter n.d.). The responsiveness of academic institutions to state pressures is in direct proportion to their political and financial vulnerability. Especially vulnerable colleges and universities are likely to pursue joint ventures with industry, whether or not they have the necessary personnel and equipment to achieve results.

Leadership

The active involvement and commitment of university and corporate leaders are crucial to forming any type of relationship (Day 1985; Gilley 1986; Gold and Charner 1986). As political pressure mounts to encourage an academic role in economic development, the active support of college and university presidents is particularly crucial. Also important is an understanding of specific institutional needs and whether or not a specific relationship is consistent with academic and corporate missions. Correct assessment of institutional capacity to contribute to successful liaisons is also fundamental (Public Policy Center 1986; Rosenzweig and Turlington 1982).

In forming liaisons to enhance economic development, industries are more likely to work with academic institutions whose leadership supports faculty entrepreneurship (Public Policy Center 1986). Industry is also attracted to academic institutions whose leaders and faculty actively pursue connections with industry. Academic leaders' willingness to establish alternative organizational arrangements can also be a key to successful implementation of industry-university alliances (Chmura 1987; Public Policy Center 1986). Finally, academic institutions with well-defined strategies for achieving liaisons with industry are more likely to attract industrial partners (Chmura 1987).

Culture and mission

In general, academic institutions and industry have distinct cultures, which are reflected by differences in mission, methods of operation, and attitudes of personnel. The lack of mutual understanding of these cultural differences can make implementation of liaisons problematic (Baaklini, Worthley, and Apfel 1979).

Mission. Perceived compatibility of mission(s), or at least an overlap of certain goals, is a key to formation of industry-university alliances (Gold and Charner 1986; Peters and Fusfeld 1983). Although some commentators argue that contractual mechanisms can ameliorate these differences (e.g., Hutt 1983; Matthews and Norgaard 1984; Tatel and Guthrie 1983), conflicts in mission are difficult to resolve for two reasons. First, academic missions are complex and often contradictory. An academic institution must balance many missions at the same time, including education and training, research and scholarship, and service (Dressel 1987; Geiger 1986). Given scarce resources, academic institutions find it difficult to pursue distinct missions with equal fervor or to choose between them. Thus, a corporation and a university may find an overlap of mission in one area, say medical research, that directly conflicts with other academic missions, such as instruction (Fairweather n.d.).

Second, industry and academe have contrasting purposes. One desires to produce and disseminate knowledge, while the other seeks to make a profit (David 1982; Peters and Fusfeld 1983). Universities are more likely to focus on basic research and open publication of research results, whereas industry emphasizes product development and proprietary rights (Praeger and Omenn 1980).

As the boundaries between academe and industry overlap—for example, through accredited corporate degree programs and shared continuing education for professionals—these underlying differences become less distinct and spanning the boundary between business and higher education through contractual vehicles becomes easier. This situation is particularly true for academic institutions that are responding to pressures from state governments to pursue goals (Chmura 1987; Public Policy Center 1986). Such changes in institutional behavior and motivation also have implications for more traditional goals, such as academic instruction and service. For example, to develop for-profit ventures, universities sometimes obtain capital from existing programs, which can deteriorate (Fairweather n.d.).

Methods of operation. For most academic institutions, the responsibility for academic activities lies with the faculty. Faculty carry out research and instruction, publish, advise students, and supervise theses and dissertations. In most institutions, faculty have substantial influence on the outcome of decisions about tenure and promotion. By placing substantial authority in the faculty, academic institutions decentralize many key decisions —in contrast with corporations, which have hierarchical, top-down decision-making structures (Praeger and Omenn 1980).

The time framework for completing tasks also varies substantially between academe and industry. Universities have a long-term view of faculty research, assuming that at some point practical applications of the results of basic research will benefit society. In contrast, to achieve or maintain profitability, industry cannot afford a significant lag time between basic research and application (Peters and Fusfeld 1983).

Conflicting management styles and time references can also adversely affect liaisons between business and higher education. Industrial accounting systems, for example, require allocation of cost by specific project and activity. This scheme is inconsistent with colleges and universities, where faculty play so many roles as to make the assignment of time to specific projects and activities inaccurate—if not impossible. A corporation might not want to deal with the complexities of academic accounting systems.

The implications of differing methods of operation for forming liaisons are twofold. First, corporations already similar in management style to universities, such as decentralized scientific companies, might find it easier to form alliances with academic institutions. Second, innovative organizational structures, such as organized research units, might be used to preserve the integrity of the parent organizations while permitting the use of innovative management techniques (Friedman and Friedman 1984, 1985; Ikenberry and Friedman 1972; Teich 1982).

Attitudes of personnel. Mutual respect of potential partners is crucial to establishing industry-university relationships (Branscomb 1984). At the institutional level, the prestige of the college or university affects its acceptability as a partner to industry. Industry often ignores community colleges as potential partners, for example, because of their perceived low status. Ironically, community colleges are often in the best position to provide technical training, which is a major industrial need (Day 1985). At the individual level, cultural and motivational differences may cause individuals on both sides to distrust each other. For example, industrial scientists working under time constraints may not trust faculty to take a deadline seriously (Peters and Fusfeld 1983; Praeger and Omenn 1980).

Establishing some form of contact between potential partners before negotiating a partnership may alleviate or reduce attitudinal barriers. The evidence suggests that prior experience enhances the mutual understanding of potential participants (Branscomb 1984, p. 45).

Academic freedom

A major tenet of academe is that faculty control the selection of research topics and the methods of conducting research. The concept of "academic freedom" also includes the obligation to encourage the free flow of information through publication and a variety of other mechanisms (Ashford 1983; Caldert 1983). Several commentators cite the potential for conflict between industry-university liaisons and academic freedom. Concern has been raised about the choice and focus of research topics (Ashford 1983; Buchbinder and Newson 1985; Caldert 1983; Hutt 1983; National Academy of Sciences 1983; Peters and Fusfeld 1983; Wofsy 1986) and about trends encouraging secrecy and proprietary rights versus open publication of research results (Blumenthal et al. 1986; Fowler 1982–83, 1984; Hutt 1983; Johnson 1984; Kenney 1986; Peters and Fusfeld 1983; Richter 1984).

The perception of whether or not industry-university relationships threaten academic freedom can be ideologically motivated. Opponents argue that the threat to academic freedom threatens the basic missions of the university:

The concept of academic freedom defines the university's responsibility to choose its research endeavors on the basis of relative academic merit. The concept of public need, in turn, defines the university's responsibility to temper this choice with a concern for the interests of the greater public good. When funds for a project come from industry investment, the university accepts an inevitable constraint on its ability to fulfill either of these expectations (Caldert 1983, p. 29).

Others argue that academic freedom is an illusory ideal, threatened and influenced as much by federally funded research as by funds from industry. Consider the following example comparing the behavior of faculty returning from a visit to a federal sponsor with faculty working on industrially funded research:

When the group's research leader returned from Washington, the scientists not only changed the title of the grant proposal that had occasioned her visit, but also rewrote a substantial part of its content. . . . When a representative of industry did not respond enthusiastically to a scientist's results, he began to pursue alternative procedures (Knorr-Cetina 1981, p. 82).

From this perspective, faculty operate in an environment constantly challenged by external audiences, only one of which is industry.

Whether real or perceived, potential threats to academic freedom affect the likelihood of a college's or university's entering into an alliance with industry. For this reason, a significant proportion of the literature on industry-university liaisons is devoted to the legal and contractual protection of academic freedom.

Legal issues

Industry-university relationships are affected by tax policy, antitrust regulations, and patent laws (Association of American Universities 1986; Peters and Fusfeld 1983). As one example, the Patent and Trademark Amendments of 1980 encouraged the transfer of technology from academe to industry by permitting universities to patent inventions derived from federally funded research projects (Association of American Universities 1986).

In addition, the resolution of conflicting legal positions through contractual means is a prerequisite to establishing industry-university liaisons, particularly research relationships. These legal issues concern patent rights, copyrights, royalties, and other intellectual property rights; commingling of industrial and federal research funds; and use of the corporate or university name (Fowler 1982–83; Hutt 1983; Johnson 1984; National Academy of Sciences 1983; Peters and Fusfeld 1983; Richter 1984).

Some university administrators must consider the legal questions involved in taking equity in for-profit organizations (Peters and Fusfeld 1983, p. 112). Others must examine alternative policies to govern potential conflicts of interest resulting from faculty entrepreneurship (Fowler 1984; Johnson 1984; Kenney 1986; Wofsy 1986).

Potential rewards

With the exception of philanthropic activities, corporations motivated by short-term results will seek an alliance with a college or colleges only if the likelihood of potential benefit for the corporation is high (Praeger and Omenn 1980). Smaller companies without substantial resources, for example, cannot afford to speculate vast sums with little certainty of positive benefits.

Similarly, universities cannot afford to invest sizable amounts in large-scale research operations unless the potential benefit is relatively certain. Some academics argue that universities cannot afford sizable investments in basic research, regardless of the potential payoff (Muller 1982). When assessing the potential benefits of liaisons with industry, universities must also take into account the reluctance of industry to pay overhead fees (Fowler 1984; Peters and Fusfeld 1983).

The concept of reward or benefit is important in assessing the impact and effectiveness of relationships between business and higher education. Particularly problematic are more elusive future-oriented goals, such as product development and spinoff companies, where the potential return on investment is difficult to estimate.

A key to effective operation of industry-university relationships is the ability of a college or university to develop and support nontraditional organizational structures.

Keys to Successful Operation

Several additional conditions are necessary for industry-university liaisons to operate smoothly once they are established. These conditions are addressed at three levels: academe, industry, and the characteristics of the relationship. As yet, little evidence links operational effectiveness with achievement of desired outcomes, particularly for research relationships focused on economic development as a goal. For this reason, the relationship between conditions affecting operations and the achievement of goals is speculative.

Academe

Seven academic issues are related to the effective operation of liaisons with industry: leadership, organizational structure, contractual mechanisms and institutional policies, capacity and resources, the faculty reward structure, faculty workload, and communication.

Leadership. Institutional leadership is needed to provide necessary resources, create innovative organizational structures, resolve faculty issues, and develop communication networks. Leadership is also important at the project or program level. Industry-university research relationships, for example, work best when the project leader is a respected scientist *and* a strong manager who believes in the usefulness of the research (Peters and Fusfeld 1983, pp. 41–42).

Organizational structure. For industry, time constraints are an important consideration in addressing training and research needs (Brazziel 1981a; Day 1985, pp. 22–23). The interdisciplinary nature of much industrial research is also an important consideration. Neither condition meshes easily with the departmental structure of academic institutions. For this reason, a key to effective operation of industry-university relationships is the ability of a college or university to develop and support nontraditional organizational structures (Baaklini, Worthley, and Apfel 1979; Chmura 1987; Geiger 1988; Gilley 1986; Johnson and Tornatzky 1981; Public Policy Center 1986). Included are organized research units, which run the gamut from traditional academic department-like structures to externally funded institutes that focus completely on research (Friedman and Friedman 1985; Teich 1982) and the use of nonprofit organizations and venture capital firms to assist in technology transfer (Gilley 1986).

The placement of an industry-university liaison within the academic institution might affect the behavior of participants (Gold and Charner 1986). Because placement in a department-like structure might not sufficiently reinforce interdisciplinary or applied research activities, many industry-university research relationships are placed in units less dependent on traditional academic goals (Chmura 1987). For example, establishing units that deemphasize instruction might encourage faculty to devote more time to applied research. Such alternatives might incorporate nonacademic staff and technicians as well as faculty and students.

Contractual mechanisms and institutional policies. Contractual mechanisms consistent with both corporate and academic norms make the success of a joint venture more likely. Such mechanisms might include specific provisions for protecting both parties by delaying but eventually permitting publication of research results. Clear guidelines for expectations for faculty behavior, from the perspective of both contractual obligations and university policy, are useful (Powers et al. 1988). Clarification of the impact of university policy, including the identification and resolution of potential conflicts of interest, is imperative (Government-University-Industry Research Roundtable and Industrial Research Institute 1988).

Capacity and resources. The key to any industry-university relationship is the quality of the participating faculty and the stature of relevant academic programs (Day 1985; Fusfeld 1983; Geiger 1988; Government-University-Industry Research Roundtable 1986; Johnson 1984; Praeger and Omenn 1980). Such expertise and visibility are inevitably linked with the productivity of the relationship and the credibility of results.

Expertise alone, however, is not sufficient. The match between faculty members' fields of expertise and the focus of the industry-university partnership is also important. In addition, sufficient numbers of faculty, students, and support staff to address the variety of activities in the relationship are essential.

Many industry-university liaisons also depend heavily on the resources of the academic institution (Praeger and Omenn 1980), including the library, laboratories, and other facilities. Finally, substantial internal funds often are needed to assist project staff in carrying out activities (Public Policy Center 1986). These requirements restrict the potential pool of university participants in large-scale research relationships with industry to a small number of institutions.

Faculty reward structure. Inherent in the concept of "faculty" is the assumption that instruction, research, and service are part of each position, embodied in each individual faculty member. Although different types of institutions place different emphases on each type of activity, the underlying philosophy is that instruction, research, and service are compatible and supportive (Bowen and Schuster 1986; Study Group 1984). The belief that research and instruction are positively correlated is especially strong:

> *It is the special function of the university to combine education with research, and knowledgeable observers believe that this combination has distinct advantages both for teaching and for science and scholarship. . . . Without the marriage of teaching and research that universities uniquely provide, the conduct of scholarly inquiry and scientific investigation. . .would be unlikely to continue at the level of quality achieved over the past two generations* (Bok 1982, p. 10).

The faculty reward structure, however, does not reinforce each behavior equally. Research and publication dominate decisions about tenure and promotion at doctorate-granting institutions (Tuckman 1979, p. 169). Externally funded research is a particularly valuable commodity in the academic marketplace (Wofsy 1986, p. 481). These criteria are also increasingly emphasized at other four-year institutions (Bowen and Schuster 1986; Boyer 1987; Cole 1982). With the exception of many community colleges, service activities are the least valued in the academic reward structure (Crosson 1986, p. 119). Concern exists that the undervalued worth of instruction and service adversely affects academic institutions:

> *Although different institutions place different emphases on research, teaching, and service in their personnel decisions, it is clear that the reward structure can act as an incentive— or as a disincentive—for quality instruction. While research can and should be mutually supportive and complementary, many of our colleges and universities overemphasize research and minimize quality teaching in personnel decisions, and this tradition has potentially damaging effects on student learning and development* (Study Group 1984, p. 59).

Several commentators have argued that substantial changes in this reward structure are required to enhance the effectiveness of industry-university liaisons (Baaklini, Worthley, and Apfel 1979; Hambrick and Swanson 1979; Johnson and Tornatzky 1981; Lynton and Elman 1987; Smith 1986). This argument assumes that liaisons between business and higher education have a common purpose, which is not supportable. To the extent that industry-university relationships emphasize research avenues consistent with existing faculty behavior, the faculty reward structure *reinforces* the relationship. Similarly, the acquisition of industrial funding for research is consistent with the current reward structure. In this context, the industry-university alliance is another stimulus for faculty to pursue research activities.

Industry-university research relationships that emphasize product development and technology transfer, however, may be inconsistent with collegiate reward structures, particularly if such activities are viewed as service rather than research related (Feller 1988, p. 27). Economic development is vulnerable in this context:

> *Economic development activities are much more likely to be added to the already long and growing list of desirable public-service activities to which academe pays lip service but which everyone on the inside knows occupies a distant third place in the hierarchy of institutional values* (Crosson 1986, p. 119).

Additional incentives might be required to increase faculty participation in these types of arrangements.

Alliances between business and higher education that emphasize training and education also run counter to the prevailing reward structure at most institutions. Such arrangements probably require some adjustment in the reward structure to encourage faculty participation, although similar arguments have been made about faculty involvement in any instructional activity (e.g., Study Group 1984).

Faculty workload. The simultaneous pursuit of research and scholarship, teaching and advising, and service requires a substantial commitment of time. After a certain point, perhaps 60 hours a week, additional activities either cannot be accommodated or must replace existing commitments (Bowen and Schuster 1986). This workload can restrict faculty involvement in industry-university alliances (Johnson 1984). When faculty involvement in collaborative arrangements is consistent with the academic reward structure, faculty may be motivated to incorporate these additional activities into their work schedules. Activities perceived as less important probably will be avoided. Again, economic development may fall into the latter category:

Colleges and universities asking their faculty for greater involvement in economic development activities, whatever they may be, should be willing to have other activities displaced and ideally should be willing to tell faculty what areas can be dropped (Crosson 1986, p. 119).

Communication. Well-established communication links with industry, state and federal governments, and regional economic development agencies enable industry-university arrangements to function more effectively (Baaklini, Worthley, and Apfel 1979; Day 1985; Peters and Fusfeld 1983). These networks better enable colleges and corporations to match personnel on specific projects and to enhance the likelihood of successful transfer of technology (Chmura 1987).

Complementary internal networks also are useful. A highly visible administrative office responsible for technology transfer and patent development, for example, might increase faculty members' identification of potential applications of their research efforts.

Industry
Beyond the requirements of leadership, capacity and resources, and communication networks that they share with academic institutions, corporations with an ability to incorporate new knowledge rapidly are more likely to benefit from collaborative arrangements with colleges and universities (Feller 1988, p. 14). Companies with decentralized, scientist-oriented structures also might find collaboration easier and more effective.

Characteristics of the relationship
In addition to the special contributions of each partner, certain characteristics of a collaborative agreement seem related to successful operation. Some evidence suggests that collaboration throughout the operation of an agreement is related to its success, including mutual determination of research topics, educational agendas, and so on (Day 1985, pp. 21–22).

Agreements based on an accurate assessment of capabilities also seem more likely to operate effectively. As an example, comprehensive colleges and universities have been more successful in relationships focused on regional economic development than have research universities. The latter are better suited to relationships centered on improving the state of the art in research (Feller 1988; Public Policy Center 1986).

Less certain are claims about the compatibility of the relationship with the existing goals, needs, and capabilities of each partner. Some authors claim that such compatibility is essential to effective industry-university liaisons (e.g., Johnson and Tornatzky 1981, pp. 51–53). The effectiveness of a research relationship, for example, may depend on the "consistency [of the relationship] with a firm's internal capabilities to assimilate new knowledge, and with individual faculty/university standards for promotion and tenure and pursuit of academic status" (Feller 1988, p. 14). Similarly, industry-university partnerships easily incorporated into university doctoral degree program requirements are more likely to operate successfully (Branscomb 1984, p. 45).

At the same time, many relationships do *not* mesh easily with the goals, needs, or capabilities of either partner. The need on either or both sides may be sufficient to search for some sort of accommodation, but the overlap of interests and needs may be small. This conflict is recognized by the substantial literature calling for adaptability and change by universities to accommodate relations with industry (e.g., Bach and Thornton 1983; Hutt 1983; Johnson and Tornatzky 1981; Lynton and Elman 1987; National Science Board 1986; National Science Foundation 1982b; Public Policy Center 1986; Schuh 1986; Stauffer 1979). In these types of relationships, retention of existing mores and operating procedures may be more difficult. For example, some partnerships have conflicted with universities' doctoral program requirements by requiring substantial delays in the submission of dissertations (Richter 1984).

These differences in perspective are reflected in differing opinions about the importance of management techniques in successfully forming and operating industry-university partnerships.

The Importance of Management: Two Views
In establishing and operating industry-university relationships, the dominant perspective in the literature is that differences between academe and industry can be resolved through careful contractual and management mechanisms. Contractual agreements can be used to resolve disputes about patents, address conflicts over proprietary rights, and ensure the university's autonomy (Broad 1982). In effect, the contract becomes the mechanism for ensuring the overlap of corporate and academic interests (Blumenthal et al. 1986; Bok 1982; Broad 1982; Fow-

Entrepreneurship and Higher Education   55

ler 1982–83, 1984; Hutt 1983; Matthews and Norgaard 1984; Powers et al. 1988; Reams 1986; Tatel and Guthrie 1983; Varrin and Kukich 1985).

A few commentators disagree, claiming that the basic dissimilarities between academe and industry in mission and culture make the resolution of crucial differences through contractual devices unlikely (Caldert 1983; Knorr-Cetina 1981). One national association has recognized the cultural, not contractual, basis underlying successful liaisons:

> *Perhaps the soundest safeguard [of the integrity of the university] is the integrity of the scientists buttressed by codes of ethics and standards of behavior advocated by faculties and institutions* (National Academy of Sciences 1983, p. 12).

Another observer argues that contractual provisions alone do not guarantee consistency of industry-university research relationships with academic instructional goals. For example, a contract that guarantees freedom to publish *and* provides for faculty release time to pursue entrepreneurial activities may be consistent with academic freedom but not with instructional goals (Fairweather n.d.).

When the broad array of factors affecting implementation and operation of industry-university liaisons is considered, including the importance of organizational structure, leadership, capacity and resources, quality of faculty, history, and culture, arguments that grant overriding importance to legal issues are unconvincing. By minimizing or ignoring the importance of additional factors, the "management school of thought" does a disservice to academic and industrial leaders pondering future alliances by oversimplifying the requirements for successful liaisons. Enlightened contractual provisions are necessary but not sufficient conditions for industry-university liaisons to achieve anticipated results.

COMPATIBILITY WITH ACADEMIC FUNCTIONS

The debate about industry-university liaisons reflects contrasting views of the nature of academic institutions, their role in society, and their ability to enhance the competitiveness of the American economy. These fundamental disagreements are obfuscated by the focus of the debate, which has been on narrow contractual issues like protection of property rights. Nevertheless, as colleges and universities evolve, a central question remains: What type of academic institutions will emerge? On one hand, certain liaisons with industry might make colleges and universities more responsive to external needs, which can benefit society. On the other hand, some partnerships with industry, perhaps even the same ones, may deemphasize instruction and decrease program quality, which may result in a net cost to society.

Judgment about the costs and benefits of industry-university alliances necessarily depends on how one views academe. Perhaps some boundaries, however, can be placed on estimating costs and benefits. Irrespective of philosophical orientation, continued pursuit of the same type of mission—research and scholarship—by more and more academic institutions *regardless of capacity or historical mission* is not desirable. Evidence indicates that as more and more universities attempt to advance along the same prestige ladder, the functions that they emphasize grow smaller and more homogeneous. High prestige is associated with research and scholarly publication; undergraduate instruction and public service are on the losing side (Bowen and Schuster 1986; Study Group 1984). In this sense, the responsiveness of academe *as a whole* needs to improve.

On the other side, alliances that detract from instruction as a primary academic mission are not helpful:

> If undergraduate instruction is a major goal (even if not the primary one), a university should pursue liaisons with industry only if it is assured that instruction will in some way benefit (or at least not be harmed) (Fairweather n.d.).

At the very least, the benefits to industry and to academic research capacity must be weighed against the costs to a variety of other academic missions, especially instruction.

Finally, the line should be drawn at university-developed for-profit ventures, especially those funded from current operating budgets and incorporated into the existing academic structure. Although the list of such ventures is expanding, little attention

Continued pursuit of the same type of mission—research and scholarship—by more and more academic institutions regardless of capacity or historical mission is not desirable.

has been paid to the compatibility of "corporate behavior" with academic values. Even the most liberal definition of "academic institution" precludes making profitability the principal objective. Indeed, profit motivation is inconsistent with the nonprofit tax status of most postsecondary institutions.

The Evidence

Evidence about the compatibility of industry-university liaisons with academic functions is slightly more substantial than data on the effectiveness of such relationships, although it is still largely anecdotal and speculative. In describing the impact on colleges and universities, most commentators fail to distinguish between the different types of liaisons between business and higher education, which include philanthropic relationships, research and technology transfer agreements, and alliances based on education, training, and professional development. The implicit assumption of homogeneity is not supportable and masks the variety of impacts resulting from industry-university relationships.

In addition to type of liaison, for academic institutions the real or potential impact of relations with industry varies by institutional focus. For this section, relevant foci are the academic missions, including research, instruction, and service, and the evolution of the institution.

The Missions: Research and Scholarship

Two generic types of industry-university liaisons can affect academic research and scholarship: philanthropic relationships and research and technology transfer agreements. Philanthropic relationships, including corporate donations of unrestricted funds and of facilities, can enhance the strength of academic research. Unrestricted funds are most desirable, as reflected in the large-scale efforts by academic institutions to pursue corporate gifts (Harris 1988).

More controversial is the compatibility of various research and technology transfer relationships, particularly large-scale agreements, with academic research and scholarship. Commentators strongly disagree about the costs and benefits of such relationships for academic research.

Potential benefits

The potential benefits for academic research and scholarship resulting from liaisons with industry concern resources, facilities, and strengthening existing programs.

Resources. In some disciplines, such as biotechnology, academic institutions could not have initiated research without substantial support from industry (Brooks 1984; Kenney 1986). Industrial funds for academic research also have enabled colleges and universities to continue research programs that otherwise might be closed:

> *But while industrial funding does* not *have the potential to replace federal funding* as the major source of financing university research, *it* does *have the potential to replace much of what universities have* lost *(and stand to lose) because of decreases in the level of federal funding* (Fowler 1982–83, p. 516).

This effect is probably limited to specific disciplines because the total ration of federal funding for academic research to funding from industry is approximately 10:1 (National Science Board 1987).

From the faculty's perspective, industrial funding may provide additional benefits. The process of applying to obtain research funds from industry can be less complicated than that of federal sponsors. Less red tape is involved in most industrially funded projects than in federally funded research (Richter 1984, p. 6).

Long-term funding from industry can also benefit faculty by freeing them from spending time pursuing additional research funds (Mai 1984, p. 3). If such funding is relatively unrestricted, faculty are likely to value the support whether or not the amount is substantial (Richter 1984, p. 26).

Facilities. Real expenditures on academic facilities have declined in the past decade (Business–Higher Education Forum 1984, p. 2). During this time, federal research and development funding for academe has not increased appreciably (National Science Foundation 1984a, p. 6, 1985d, p. 5). The result has been a substantial deterioration of academic science and engineering facilities (Mai 1984; National Research Council 1985b; Peters and Fusfeld 1983).

By providing faculty with access to modern equipment and facilities, some industry-university partnerships enhance the productivity of faculty and save the university a substantial investment in money (Larsen and Wigand 1987, p. 589). At the same time, industrial scientists may benefit by gaining access to some equipment not available in their work setting.

Strengthening existing programs. Critics argue that industry-university research agreements can distort the direction of academic research. Although this conflict is serious (see the following discussion), the criticism is overly simplistic. In some agreements, industry funds faculty to continue existing research projects. In this context, industrial funding can strengthen existing research programs. The key is the match between the research needs of industry, existing faculty activities, and the freedom faculty have to continue or drop particular lines of inquiry.

Potential costs

The potential costs to academic research and scholarship concern six issues: academic freedom, focus of research, secrecy, faculty productivity, intellectual property rights, and the split between the haves and the have nots.

Academic freedom. Many commentators argue that academic freedom, or the freedom of faculty to choose research topics and methods of investigation, is potentially threatened by industry-university research partnerships (Ashford 1983; Caldert 1983; National Academy of Sciences 1983; Tatel and Guthrie 1983). Of particular concern is the selection of research topics to fit the sponsor's goals rather than the faculty member's interests (Buchbinder and Newson 1985, p. 51; Wofsy 1986, p. 485).

To examine the potential impact on academic freedom, consider the categories of choice in any research project. They include the category of research (a continuum of basic to applied), the specific project, the methodology, the method of evaluation, and the approach to dissemination. Factors influencing these choices include personal interest, availability of funding, desire for future funding, and the acceptability of the research to the academic community (Ashford 1983, pp. 20–22). Industrial sponsors can use the availability of current and future research funds to influence academic research in any category of choice. Beyond the obvious influence of providing funds for research on a specific topic, more subtle influences also take place:

Take the case of a toxicologist who has reason to believe that two chemicals could be significant human carcinogens, but who has the resources to pursue a study of only one. If she knows that chemical A is manufactured by a company that is about to give a large technology/development grant to her university, and that chemical B is not, will her choice be unaffected by that fact? Is it not fair to say that fear of upsetting a potential funder may provide an incentive to investigate B rather than A? (Ashford 1983, p. 22).

The freedom of faculty to choose research topics may be particularly threatened in departments where a single corporation provides the majority of research funds (Kenney 1986).

The evidence, although limited, lends credence to these concerns. Selection of a research topic is clearly influenced by industrial funding in biotechnology (Blumenthal et al. 1986, pp. 1364–65) and in other disciplines (Fowler 1984, p. 37). A study of industry-university liaisons in microelectronics also supports these findings:

Industrial researchers unilaterally determined the nature of the research half of the time, and university researchers cooperated with industry researchers in defining research goals in other cases. There were no cases reported in which university researchers defined research goals alone (Larsen and Wigand 1987, p. 589).

Some commentators disagree with this evidence, claiming that *any* externally funded research influences the choice of·research topic (Knorr-Cetina 1981, p. 82; Richter 1984, p. 29). Others argue that increasing research funds from industry lessens dependence on federal sources, which increases faculty's choice (Rosenzweig and Turlington 1982).

Is industry-supported research distinct in its influence from other sources of external funding? For academic freedom, the crucial factor is whether or not the sponsor *requires* the research project to focus on specific approaches, topics, and outcomes (Knorr-Cetina 1981, p. 90). Although not true for all relationships, it appears that industry is more likely than other sponsors to fund research with a focus on specific applications, often with a time-specific commercial focus. In such cases, industrially funded projects are less compatible with academic freedom than those supported by other sources of funding.

The focus of research: Basic versus applied. Unlike academic freedom, little disagreement exists about the generic focus of research funded by industry: Irrespective of discipline, the emphasis is on applied, not basic, research (Ashford 1983; Blumenthal et al. 1986; Branscomb 1984; Hutt 1983; Larsen and Wigand 1987; Peters and Fusfeld 1983; Richter 1984; Tatel and Guthrie 1983; Wofsy 1986). The emphasis on application, including commercial applicability, sometimes is specified in the research agreement. The Washington University/Monsanto Corporation agreement, for example, stipulates that two-thirds of the funds go to applied research and the remainder to basic research (Kenney 1986, pp. 67–68). One commentator claims that the research direction of an entire discipline can be affected if it is highly dependent on corporate funding (Kenney 1986, pp. 112–13).

In some disciplines, particularly engineering, the line between applied and basic is arbitrarily drawn. When such ambiguity exists, the potential incompatibility of industry-funded research is less evident:

> *Even when industrial contracts are focused on practical problems, they sometimes provide occasions for digging more deeply into fundamental questions* (Richter 1984, p. 5).

On the whole, the applied focus of industry-university research liaisons seems incompatible with many academic research goals, especially for basic research that has a long- rather than short-term focus.

Secrecy. A major academic tenet is that scientific progress depends on open publication of research results and the free flow of information. The proprietary nature of some industry-funded research may conflict with this central belief (Kenney 1986; National Academy of Sciences 1983).

Although piecemeal, the evidence suggests that secrecy is a major problem with some industry-university research relationships. One survey found that academic administrators were concerned about the emphasis on secrecy and its impact on faculty behavior (Fowler 1984, p. 37). More specific results were found in a survey of biotechnology faculty. Industrially funded projects in biotechnology are likely to include restrictions on publication, including delays in and prohibition of open release of research results. Biotechnology faculty working on industrially funded research projects also interact less frequently with their colleagues, thereby further restricting the free flow of information (Blumenthal et al. 1986, pp. 1364–65).

Faculty productivity. Some critics argue that faculty involved in industrially funded research may decrease their productivity, particularly those interested in commercial gain (see, e.g., Wofsy 1986). The only study to address this question directly, a survey of biotechnology faculty, contradicts this assertion, however. Biotechnology faculty receiving support from industry had more publications, filed for more patents, and developed more inventions than their colleagues who were not supported by industry (Blumenthal et al. 1986, p. 1363). Because faculty receiving support from industry also receive more funding from all external sources (Richter 1984), receipt of industrial support is best viewed as one of several indications of faculty productivity.

Intellectual property rights. A substantial portion of the literature about industry-university relationships emphasizes the conflict between the two parties over intellectual property rights (patents and copyrights). The contractual bases for resolving such differences are, however, increasingly well understood (Reams 1986). Although the contractual issues are complex and must address the specific circumstances of the partners, such conflicts are resolvable in part because of their visibility. Less obvious conflicts, such as changes in faculty activities, are much more difficult to resolve contractually (Ashford 1983, p. 18).

The haves and the have nots. Industrial support for academic research is concentrated in a small number of institutions ("Business and Universities" 1982; Drew 1985; National Science Board 1985). On a national level, this pattern of differential support has two principal consequences for academic institutions. It assists in maintaining the viability of research universities by making them less vulnerable to fluctuations in federal funding (Rosenzweig and Turlington 1982). At the same time, it reinforces the second-class status of other four-year institutions (Business–Higher Education Forum 1984; Drew 1985). The gulf between these types of institutions is worrisome because approximately half of all undergraduates and graduates in engineering are trained at these less prestigious institutions (National Science Foundation 1984b, 1985a, 1985b). Failure to expose a larger proportion of scientists and engineers to the latest research techniques and equipment may also reduce the national capacity for research (Drew 1985).

The Missions: Instruction and Advising

Unlike research and scholarship, little attention has been paid to the impact of industry-university liaisons on academic instruction (Fairweather n.d.). Two surveys of academic administrators to elicit concerns about the compatibility of industrial relationships with academic functions failed to elicit a single response related to instruction (Fowler 1984; Peters and Fusfeld 1983).

To ameliorate this lack of attention to instruction, this section examines the potential benefits and costs of industry-university philanthropic, education and training, and research relationships for academic instruction.

Potential benefits

The potential benefits for academic instruction resulting from liaisons with industry concern recruiting and retaining students and faculty and the instructional environment.

Recruiting and retaining students. Corporate contributions of scholarships can increase students' access, particularly for those who otherwise could not afford a college education. Scholarships can also increase access for specific groups, including minorities.

Industry-university research relationships also provide incentives for students to enroll and remain in college programs. Research liaisons that provide students with access to industrial laboratories can assist universities in attracting students. Industrially funded research that includes student stipends can encourage retention. The opportunity to gain vocational experience while pursuing a degree and the increased likelihood of job placement are also attractive to potential students (Richter 1984, p. 22). This factor is especially important for graduate programs in science and engineering, where the financial incentive for bachelor's recipients to enter industry rather than to continue studies has resulted in a shortage of American-born doctoral students (Babco 1987; Barthel and Early 1985; National Science Board 1985; National Science Foundation 1982a; Stern and Chandler 1987).

Recruiting and retaining faculty. Throughout the 1980s, colleges and universities offering programs in high-demand technical fields have faced shortages of faculty (Barthel and Early 1985; Doigan 1984a, 1984b; National Science Foundation 1982a). The shortage has been especially acute in engineering and computer science (Doigan 1984b; Doigan and Gilkeson 1986), although recent trends show improvement (Doigan and Gilkeson 1986).

Industry-university liaisons may assist universities in resolving shortages of faculty in several ways. By endowing chairs, corporations may enhance the ability of colleges and universities to attract outstanding senior faculty. By contributing funds to supplement salaries, several corporations may have helped universities retain their junior faculty (Business–Higher Education Forum 1984; Peters and Fusfeld 1983).

Education and training relationships that encourage industrial employees to teach are helpful to many institutions (Business–Higher Education Forum 1984; Ping 1981). Many community colleges and proprietary institutions depend heavily on part-time faculty from local industry (Boyle 1983).

Research agreements may also assist academic institutions in attracting and retaining faculty. Relationships that provide access to industrial laboratories, increased opportunities for consulting, and the like assist colleges and universities in recruiting faculty (Doigan and Gilkeson 1986; Fairweather n.d.).

The instructional environment. Corporate gifts of equipment and donations for capital expenditures can enhance academic facilities and the instructional environment. Use of part-time faculty from industry can reduce student/faculty ratios and class sizes, which enhances instructional quality. And industrial employees can enhance the quality of technical programs, particularly in community colleges, by helping to keep the curriculum current (Boyle 1983).

Potential costs

Industry-university relationships can also adversely affect academic instruction. The relevant issues include lack of emphasis on undergraduate education, doctoral program processes, faculty activities, and faculty-student interaction.

Lack of emphasis on undergraduate education. Although industry-university relationships cover an array of activities, the majority of industrial funding for academe has focused on research and graduate education (Ping 1981):

Industry has given increased attention to science and engineering research and to graduate education, but private sector support of undergraduate education has not increased similarly (National Science Board 1986, pp. 1–2).

In this context, industry-university relations reinforce trends toward graduate and away from undergraduate instruction, which may exacerbate the perceived decline in undergraduate programs that has received considerable national attention (Bowen and Schuster 1986; Boyer 1987; Cole 1982; Study Group 1984).

Doctoral program processes. For industry-university research relationships, one key to compatibility with academic functions is congruence with doctoral program processes (Branscomb 1984, p. 45). The evidence, although limited, suggests that this "fit" has not been easily accomplished. Proprietary rights and secrecy can adversely affect doctoral education by preventing students from using data for dissertations and by imposing delays on submission of dissertations (Richter 1984, pp. 3–4). In one case, for example, a dissertation was delayed for one year in accordance with the research agreement (Richter 1984, p. 3). The emphasis on protecting research results can also adversely affect the quality of graduate instruction by preventing timely incorporation of results into the curriculum.

Research agreements focused on short-term product development may also conflict with doctoral program processes. To meet deadlines, many of these agreements use full-time technicians rather than graduate students, which reduces potential instructional and training benefits for students (Fairweather n.d.).

Faculty activities. Over the past two decades, engineering and science faculty have devoted more time to research and less to instruction (Maxfield 1982; National Science Foundation 1981, 1982a, 1985c). Evidence suggests that this trend has adversely affected the quality of instruction (Bowen and Schuster 1986; Boyer 1987; Study Group 1984). The National Science Board (1986), for example, reports that faculty in high-demand technical fields do not spend enough time keeping the curriculum current or advising students.

Reinforcing this trend, to compete with industry for talent, universities are offering faculty in high-demand areas greater release time and lower teaching loads (Doigan 1984b, p. 6). The emphasis of these incentives is on research, not instruction (National Science Foundation and U.S. Department of Education 1980, p. 10).

As mentioned previously, industry-university relationships focus heavily on research (National Science Board 1986; Ping 1981). As one example, the Hoechst–Massachusetts General Hospital (Harvard University) agreement specifies that participating faculty must devote most of their time to research (Kenney 1986, p. 63). By reinforcing faculty research behavior, these relationships may exacerbate existing instructional problems. Especially vulnerable are the high-demand science and engineering fields where class sizes, student/faculty ratios, and faculty workloads are already too high (Doigan 1984b; Doigan and Gilkeson 1986; National Science Foundation and U.S. Department of Education 1980, pp. 35–36).

Except for data on national trends, little evidence exists to support or contradict suppositions about the compatibility of industry-university research relationships with instructional quality. A survey of biotechnology faculty showed that faculty receiving research funds from industry did not teach less than their colleagues (Blumenthal et al. 1986, p. 1363). That study, however, did not take into account type of research relationship, including length of relationship, focus on basic or applied research, and so on. In contrast to that survey, a case study of engineering and computer science programs found a negative effect:

> The range between the "best" and "worst" industrial-funding situations, from the standpoint of university faculty committed to academic values, appears to be much wider than the range between the "best" and the "worst" government-funding situations (Richter 1984, p. 7).

This conflicting, piecemeal information is further evidence of the lack of evaluative data about the impact of industry-university agreements on faculty activities across a variety of disciplines.

Faculty-student interaction. Related to the potential for decreased time spent on instruction and advising, a variety of

By reinforcing faculty research behavior, these relationships may exacerbate existing instructional problems.

faculty-student relationships might be adversely affected by certain industry-university arrangements. Biotechnology again has received special attention:

Abuses of faculty-student relationships have drawn attention at several universities: neglect of pre- and postdoctoral trainees by "two-hat" advisers busy with commercial involvements, increasing pressure for secrecy that inhibits communication and regards colleagues as competitors, fear that thesis and research ideas will be transferred to the commercial sector and exploited (Wofsy 1986, p. 485).

The Missions: Service

The academic service function falls into the broad category of responsiveness to societal and institutional needs. Public service focuses on activities carried out for the benefit of society; institutional service focuses on assisting the academic institution in carrying out necessary functions. Academic institutions, especially public land-grant universities, have been criticized for lack of responsiveness to public service (Schuh 1986). Even private research universities can be said to have a responsibility to serve the public at large through research (Bok 1982). In this light, the primary benefit of industry-university service-oriented relationships is the university's enhanced responsiveness to societal needs:

Liaisons that require the university to consider its broader social role must surely enhance the public service function common to many universities. Such an impact would be welcomed by academics and legislators concerned that the activities of faculty in land-grant institutions have become virtually indistinguishable from their colleagues in private institutions (Fairweather n.d.).

The principal cost of these alliances is distortion and perhaps loss of traditional academic values. By expanding the role of academic service in the faculty workload, the time faculty spend on instruction and on research and scholarship will probably decline (Bowen and Schuster 1986).

In this context, compatibility (or the lack of it) has two implications. Lack of compatibility may point to the need for substantial change to fulfill the service function more effectively. It may also point to a threshold beyond which academic institutions are no longer recognizable as distinct entities. These concepts are explored more fully for the three foci of industry-university service-oriented relationships: continuing education, technology transfer, and additional economic development.

Continuing education

Business–higher education liaisons formed to foster continuing education, especially when based on degree programs and formal courses, are clearly compatible with the academic mission of service. Indeed, some argue that continuing education is the primary academic mechanism for responding to societal needs (e.g., Cross 1981). Continuing education programs that focus on training and vocational preparation are compatible with many types of academic institutions. Job training and retraining appear most compatible with the mission of the community college; doctorate-granting universities seem better suited to upgrade the training of professionals in high-demand technical fields.

Although compatible with academic service, continuing education is less compatible with the academic reward structure (Stark, Lowther, and Hagerty 1986). Although the use of non-traditional faculty in continuing education programs long has been accepted practice (Houle 1980), to update professionals in such specialized fields as superconductivity requires the involvement of full-time faculty from major research universities (Public Policy Center 1986). For these faculty, service has the least value in the reward structure (Crosson 1986).

Technology transfer

The compatibility of industry-university technology transfer agreements with academic functions varies by mechanism. Mechanisms consistent with traditional academic practices are the most compatible: conferences, publications, extension programs, and personnel exchange programs (Feller 1988). Some newer approaches, such as research and development limited partnerships and some forms of organized research units, are designed to enhance responsiveness in a manner consistent with academic values (Bartlett and Siena 1983–84).

Unfortunately, the evidence suggests that traditional technology transfer vehicles are ineffective (Johnson and Tornatzky 1981). And although conceptually appealing, research and development limited partnerships have yet to be shown effective, much less cost-effective.

For these reasons, approaches have been developed to encourage direct university involvement in technology transfer, including arrangements that focus on product development, creation of spinoff companies, and university-formed for-profit ventures (Baldwin and Green 1984–85; Larsen and Wigand 1987; Public Policy Center 1986). As academic institutions become more directly involved in technology transfer, the compatibility with some academic values, including academic freedom, decreases (Feller 1988, p. 31). This conflict is especially likely when technology transfer is the responsibility of tenure-track instructional faculty rather than, for example, extension faculty hired for the purpose of technology transfer. Implications for the faculty workload and the preservation of academe as an independent entity are also of concern. Finally, the large-scale applicability of these more radical technology mechanisms have yet to be proved effective or cost-effective.

Economic development
Economic development contained in industry-university relationships includes development of human capital, economic research and analysis, state-of-the-art research, enhancing the economic capacity of the local area or region, developing new companies, and increasing employment (Corporation for Penn State 1986; Public Policy Center 1986). Three of these activities are in principle compatible with academic values: the development of human capital, economic research and analysis, and advanced research. More problematic are expectations for direct economic benefits, including enhancing regional economic capacity, creating spinoff businesses, and increasing employment. As with technology transfer, the larger questions concern the type of institutions that result from pursuit of economic development, whether or not this evolution is effective, and whether the benefits outweigh the costs.

Evolution of the Institution
The compatibility of industry-university liaisons with academic functions is complex because a single relationship can *simultaneously* benefit certain academic functions while harming others. The central question is whether the overall impact, taking into account benefits *and* costs, makes the industry-university arrangement worthwhile. In this light, several institutional-level issues are of interest: faculty entrepreneurship, faculty work-

load, the structure of research, disciplinary conflicts, and the nature of academic institutions.

Faculty entrepreneurship

As evidenced in the Pajaro Dunes conference, which brought together leaders from academe and industry, faculty entrepreneurship has received increasing attention in academe (Broad 1982). Particular attention has been paid to faculty owning shares in spinoff companies and to faculty owning and managing start-up companies; less attention has been focused on more traditional activities, such as consulting. Attention also has been paid to *institutional* policy, especially policies that encourage institutional and faculty participation in equity arrangements in the pursuit of for-profit ventures (Feller 1988). As institutions evolve toward corporate behavior, their instructional and service activities may be deemphasized.

Two perspectives dominate the debate about faculty entrepreneurship. To make academic institutions more responsive to needed economic development, some commentators argue for increased administrative support for faculty entrepreneurship, recognizing the importance of individual faculty in creating the new technologically oriented companies that seem so important to the future of the economy (Gilley 1986; Public Policy Center 1986).

Others argue that faculty pursuit of commercial gain is incompatible with the pursuit of knowledge (Linnell 1982; National Academy of Sciences 1983). From this perspective, faculty who spend considerable time on external commercial interests may cease to be "faculty" in the traditional sense of the term (Fairweather n.d.; Reams 1986).

Examination of faculty entrepreneurial activities has focused on high-demand technical fields, especially biotechnology, and to a lesser degree engineering and computer science. These studies show that faculty involved extensively in the operation of companies devote less time to their academic functions (Kenney 1986; Richter 1984). Recent restrictions on faculty entrepreneurship at Washington University seem to support these research findings; apparently, faculty could not carry out their academic duties while managing commercial operations.

Faculty workload

Faculty play a wide variety of roles in academic institutions, including researcher, scholar, teacher, adviser, and provider of public service. Even for extremely productive faculty, the workload has limits: Beyond a certain point, the addition of responsibilities requires the elimination of other activities (Bowen and Schuster 1986). Industry-university relationships that overlap substantially with existing faculty activities may not affect the faculty workload significantly. Many of these relationships, however, require substantial changes in faculty behavior. When activities like economic development and technology transfer are added to the agenda, particularly in a short-term project, some traditional activities must be reduced or eliminated. Evidence suggests that service and instruction are the first to suffer, with research and scholarship less likely to be affected (Bowen and Schuster 1986; Crosson 1986).

When faculty must simultaneously pursue open and secret research agendas, the workload is further increased. In such cases, reductions in other activities may result:

> *The burden of maintaining a teaching program and two separate research programs, where the results of one research program are to be widely disseminated and the results of the other may be required to be kept secret in the pursuit of commercial success, is more than even the most responsible faculty member can be expected to shoulder* (Giamatti 1983, p. 6).

Structure of research

The location of an industrially funded research project in an academic institution has implications beyond administrative convenience. Consider an applied research project with two options for placement: a peripheral organized research unit supported by soft money and a traditional academic department. Placement in the ORU might encourage faculty involved in the project to spend more time on research than would be typical for a department-based project, which may be consistent with project research goals but may decrease faculty involvement in instruction, advising, and some service activities. Locating the project in a department might increase the likelihood that participating faculty will continue to teach but may be less effective in addressing applied research goals. Each alternative has associated costs and benefits; in either case, the location has implications beyond the scope of the research project.

A related issue concerns the operating philosophy of industry-university research agreements and the consequences for faculty behavior and academic freedom. Some agreements are based on bureaucratic structures with top-down decision making, such as projects designed for product development that require involvement by corporate sales and marketing managers. These arrangements can conflict with the academic environment where faculty make decisions about time allocation, student involvement, and so on. Research agreements requiring a top-down decision-making structure are probably best served by involving faculty through a peripheral ORU. The differences in structure and incentives in such an ORU, particularly one dependent on this type of research agreement, may be unrecognizable as an academic entity. Again, the question arises whether faculty involved in such an arrangement respond to the more comprehensive role of faculty member or to the more narrow role of project researcher.

Disciplinary conflicts

Corporate funding of academic institutions is concentrated on disciplines of importance to the corporation. Most often they are technical fields relevant to company research and production or disciplines that produce graduates hired by the company (Branscomb 1984).

The relatively narrow disciplinary focus of funds from industry has implications for academic institutions. Concern exists about the liberal arts and humanities, which already receive disproportionately fewer rewards than their more visible science and engineering counterparts (Peterson 1983). Faculty salaries in liberal arts and humanities, for example, are substantially lower than in computer science, engineering, and business (Babco 1987). Industry has provided funds for salary supplements in high-demand fields, which exacerbates salary discrepancies between disciplines (Business–Higher Education Forum 1984; Peters and Fusfeld 1983). The university may also contribute to this discrepancy by taking funds from one department to give to another group interested in forming an alliance with industry.

Disproportionate rewards, such as higher salaries, are necessary to attract faculty in high-demand technical fields. As the discrepancy between disciplines grows, the question remains whether the fabric of an academic institution is threatened:

These questions are troublesome precisely because they concern not merely budgetary items but, at a more fundamental level, the character of instructional programs, research directions, and educational mission (Matthews and Norgaard 1984, pp. 94–95).

Nature of the academic institution

Beyond the specific industry-university relationship lie the questions of what happens to the academic institution as a whole and whether such changes benefit society. As traditionally defined, academic institutions claim to benefit society mostly through indirect means, such as by training future professionals, educating the citizenry, and carrying out research that may have future applications. For the most part, even the direct economic development roles have concentrated on traditional academic strengths, such as continuing professional education. Economic benefits also have been defined in traditional ways, such as the contribution of employee tax revenues to local communities.

In contrast, the newer industry-university relationships encourage *direct* involvement in economic development through providing technical assistance, creating spinoff companies to increase employment and competitiveness, and paying greater attention to application and product development. These liaisons assume that direct involvement in economic development can be accomplished within existing institutions by modifying reward structures, values, and goals. The foci, incentives, and even missions envisioned in these modified institutions are, however, so fundamental that the resulting institutions may not be recognizable in current terms. Given financial constraints and limits on faculty workload, will the modified institutions continue to emphasize instruction and basic research? (Aslanian and Brickell 1981; Douglas 1984; Haddad 1986). Will institutions that undergo substantial revisions in mission and reward structures be able to attract the same type of faculty that were responsible for its reputation in the first place? And what kinds of decisions will the new institutions make?

Should it [the university] limit its enrollment to capable students who could assist in its research and development? Should it reduce its teaching functions in favor of research and recruit its faculty accordingly? Should it construe its service obligations as met by selling its services? Should its research and development be guided by market considera-

tions? Should it shift toward corporate forms of governance and management? (Aslanian and Brickell 1981, p. 18).

University autonomy and its importance to the effectiveness of academe are also relevant. As an example, the liaison between Whitehead and Massachusetts Institute of Technology gave Whitehead a substantial voice in decisions about hiring faculty (Kenney 1986, p. 51). The potential for conflict of interest between academic and nonacademic goals in this research relationship is high:

> *Clearly, it [the research relationship] raises the question of whether the new faculty members will be chosen to meet the university's institutional and educational needs or will be selected to meet the research needs of the Whitehead Institute* (Caldert 1983, pp. 28–29).

Although some critics argue that institutional autonomy harms economic development by decreasing academic responsiveness to the marketplace, autonomy can also *assist* economic development. Economic needs change over time, and practices that seem irrelevant one year are in high demand the next. Institutional autonomy helps ensure that the intellectual capacity will be available when needed. For example, two decades ago Johns Hopkins University closed its School of Engineering in response to a glut of engineers in the marketplace. If other institutions had followed suit, the current shortage of engineers and engineering faculty might be much worse.

Autonomy is also related to credibility. The recent example of the University of Rochester's business program denying admission to a qualified student because he worked for a rival of Eastman Kodak, the major financial contributor to the school, raised questions about the integrity of the faculty and their programs ("University of Rochester" 1987). If the university is perceived to alter its missions in the pursuit of funding, its role as a relatively disinterested producer of knowledge may be threatened (Carley 1988; Weiner 1982).

These questions and issues necessarily depend on ideology and, it is hoped, some type of evidence. In either case, industry-university relationships, both singly and cumulatively, can affect the institution as a whole.

ASSESSING THE IMPACT

In 1982, the National Science Foundation (NSF) recommended that researchers examine the impact of industry-university liaisons on undergraduate and graduate curricula, faculty activities, and academic disciplines (1982b, p. 2). These questions about impact and effectiveness remain largely unanswered. Although traditional liaisons, such as continuing education, are assessed regularly (Houle 1980), few evaluations of industry-university research relationships exist. Since 1982, NSF and other national associations increasingly have become advocates, arguing for increased links between business and higher education rather than evaluation of existing relationships (National Research Council 1985b; National Science Board 1986; National Science Foundation 1982b). For industry-university research relationships, assessment remains the missing ingredient (Business–Higher Education Forum 1988a, 1988b).

For industry-university relationships, assessment remains the missing ingredient.

Initial Considerations
The first step in evaluating industry-university research relationships is to understand their complexity and to select a focus for assessment.

Understanding the complexity
Evaluating industry-university research relationships is made difficult by the number of mechanisms used (Branscomb 1984, p. 43). These mechanisms range from small-scale technical assistance projects to large-scale, long-term collaborative research agreements. Evaluative approaches useful for one mechanism may not be applicable to another, making development of a uniform procedure problematic.

Assessment is also made complex by the range of audiences, often including state and federal government officials, industrial leaders, academic administrators, faculty, and students. These audiences can have different expectations, and they can select different criteria to judge the outcome of a research relationship.

Distinct organizational perspectives also complicate evaluation of industry-university research alliances. For example, an academic administrator expects the impact or effectiveness of a collaborative agreement to be judged differently by individuals at distinct hierarchical levels—extrainstitutional, institutional, college or school, department or program, organized research unit, project, and individual faculty and students.

Finally, evaluation is made complex by the multiple effects

resulting from the same relationship. A single collaborative agreement may benefit faculty and students in one or more ways, while harming them in others. Assessing the cumulative effect of an industry-university agreement is seldom straight-forward.

Selecting the focus

For evaluating industry-university alliances, four components are relevant: *description, impact, effectiveness,* and *cost-effectiveness.* All evaluations have a descriptive component, which includes a list of participants, their activities, and so on. Once described, information about the impact of the liaison on a variety of factors, including compatibility with academic and industrial functions, is important.

A third question concerns the effectiveness of the collabora-tive agreement: Did the agreement reach its goals? If product development was a goal, how many products were developed? If encouraging spinoff companies was an aim, how many were created? Did projects designed to enhance the training of indus-trial scientists do so?

Once questions about effectiveness are answered, one ques-tion remains: Was the liaison cost-effective? Was the invest-ment made by Monsanto Corporation in research agreements with Washington University and Harvard University, for exam-ple, a cost-effective approach to gain useful results? Cost-effectiveness applies both to the corporate partner and to the academic institution. Particularly problematic is the calculation of monetary returns in complex research relationships. Unfortu-nately, academic institutions, which have shown little inclina-tion or ability to calculate costs and benefits, often fail to consider cost-effectiveness at all.

To assess impact, effectiveness, and cost-effectiveness, the evaluation should distinguish between *direct* and *indirect* re-sults. For example, a partnership might benefit a student di-rectly by providing funds for a graduate assistantship. The corporate partner might benefit indirectly from the student's making a discovery on his or her own, quite apart from the re-search agreement. The discovery might not have occurred had the student left school for financial reasons.

Another important distinction is between *short-term* and *long-term* effects. A research agreement might result in sub-stantial short-term returns that have no long-lasting benefits for either partner. Conversely, a particular collaborative agreement may show little benefit immediately but over time demonstrate long-term benefits.

The *intent* of the assessment is also relevant. If the purpose is to improve the operation of a research agreement, a *formative assessment* is relevant. In this approach, the intent is to identify problems and make recommendations for improvements. In contrast, the intent of a *summative assessment* is to judge whether or not the industry-university relationship achieved desired results cost-effectively.

Once these distinctions are understood and appropriate choices made, the selection of audience(s), appropriate hierarchical levels, and relevant criteria follows. These choices are not easy; the alternatives are extensive. Consider the following alternative foci for an evaluation of industry-university research agreements: (1) by discipline across institutions (e.g., the overall impact of industry-university agreements on biotechnology); (2) by institution irrespective of discipline, i.e., the cumulative effect of relations with industry on an academic institution; (3) by discipline within the institution (e.g., computer science at the Pennsylvania State University); (4) comparative assessment between disciplines within an institution (e.g., direct and indirect effects of an industry-university arrangement on different departments); (5) by location in an institution (e.g., organized research unit versus department-like structure); (6) across all institutions and disciplines, i.e., national summative assessment for academic institutions; (7) by type of agreement; (8) by corporate partner; (9) by specific field within the corporate partner; (10) by field across all participating corporate partners; (11) across industry, i.e., national summative assessment for industry; (12) by state; (13) by discipline within the state; (14) by type of agreement within the state; (15) across states, i.e., national summative assessment across states; (16) by region; (17) by discipline within the region; (18) by type of agreement within the region; and (19) across regions, i.e., national summative assessment across regions.

The choice of audience, hierarchical level, summative or formative format, and so on affects the selection of criteria for the evaluation.

Criteria
Criteria for evaluating industry-university research liaisons can be classified into internal and external categories based on their relationship to the academic participant.

Internal criteria

Internal criteria focus on five areas: the research agreement, faculty, students, departments and programs, and the institution.

The research agreement. The relative importance of the goals of a research agreement determine criteria. Criteria might include development of products; attainment of patents, copyrights, and licenses; and increased professional training of participants. To determine cost-effectiveness, the value of these outcomes is compared with the total costs of investment.

Faculty. For faculty, the principal interest is the impact of the collaborative agreement on workload and activities. Outcomes might include percent of time spent on research, teaching, advising, and service both before and during participation in the research agreement; change in total workload; and number of activities added or dropped as a result of participating in the research arrangement. Perceptions of the effect on academic freedom, including choice of research topic and freedom of publication, instruction and advising, and quality of academic programs are also relevant.

Students. To assess the effect of industry-university research liaisons on graduate students, criteria would include the extent of students' participation in relevant research projects and the ability of students to complete degree programs in a timely fashion. For the few undergraduate students involved in industry-university research alliances, relevant outcomes center on instructional quality.

Departments and programs. For academic departments, the impact of industry-university alliances on graduate and undergraduate instruction is important. Criteria might include changes in faculty time spent on instruction and student-faculty interaction and the extent and types of changes in curricula. Also relevant are indications of students' having problems completing degree programs as a direct or indirect result of industry-university research relationships.

The effect on ability to recruit students and faculty also is important to heads of departments and programs. Of special importance is whether or not industry-university research agreements make a department more or less appealing to potential faculty and students.

Finally, indications of changes in program quality resulting directly or indirectly from industry-university collaborative arrangements are of interest. Indicators might include several before-and-after measurements, including reputational assessments by outside experts (e.g., Jones, Lindzey, and Coggeshall 1982a, 1982b, 1982c, 1982d; Roose and Anderson 1970) and selectivity by students (e.g., Astin and Solomon 1979). More comprehensive internal assessments might incorporate several measures of change in institutional resources, faculty members' achievements, quality of students, program efficiency, clients' satisfaction, and external reputation (Blackburn and Lingenfelter 1973; Clark, Hartnett, and Baird 1976; Fairweather 1988; Webster 1986).

The institution. The cumulative effect of industry-university research relationships, either singly or in combination, is relevant to institutional decision makers. Criteria for assessing effectiveness might include changes in expenditures for research and development, improvement in facilities, enhanced ability to recruit faculty and students, generation of new programs, and enhanced reputation of the institution and its programs.

To judge impact, institutional leaders require data about changes in procedures for granting tenure and promoting faculty; evidence of a shift in the faculty's behavior toward or away from basic research, applied research, and instruction; and complaints about conflicts with academic freedom and publication. An indication of the effectiveness of contractual procedures in resolving potential conflicts on patent rights and royalties is also relevant. Finally, determining the amount and source of internal funds invested in industry-university research agreements is important to assess the institutionwide impact of the research agreement(s).

External criteria

Most external criteria for evaluating industry-university research liaisons focus on the social and economic benefits of the relationship. Some academics have argued that the direct economic benefits of the university to society, such as through tax revenues, are substantial. When indirect social benefits, such as providing educated citizens for our democracy, are included, the contribution of academe to society is immeasurable (Bowen 1977). Others argue that the traditional concept of education as a "social good" is no longer adequate in a highly competitive international economy (Chmura, Henton, and Melville 1988).

Several models have been developed to measure the economic and social impact of academe on society, focusing on individual institutions (e.g., Lyall and Montoya 1981), states (California Postsecondary Education Commission 1984; Van Pattee 1973); and the nation (Caffrey and Isaacs 1971). Each shows a substantial positive influence of higher education on the economy, but in each case, measurement of even the most direct economic benefit is problematic, relying to a large degree on the analyst's assumptions.

Current economic pressures have led many interested parties to judge industry-university research liaisons by their immediate economic impact (Brooks 1984, p. 20). One focus is the impact of the collaborative arrangement on the work force, such as evidence of upgraded training, academic programs modified in response to changes in the economy, and production of graduates in relevant fields. For some relationships, the number of products developed is the principal measure of success. For others, creation of spinoff companies and increased employment are standards for success. The Ben Franklin Partnership in Pennsylvania, for example, specifies three measures of success: (1) the creation and maintenance of jobs in Pennsylvania, (2) improved business productivity, and (3) diversification of the state's economy by creating new high-technology companies and attracting industry from other states (Corporation for Penn State 1986).

This emphasis on short-term economic impact seems inappropriate and unrealistic. Assessing the societal benefits of colleges and universities is difficult because academic institutions have multiple missions, many with a long-term focus. It is mainly in the long run that evidence of the economic and social benefits of investing in higher education is clear (Rosenzweig and Turlington 1982), requiring evaluations of industry-university research relationships to incorporate a historical perspective.

Consider two examples of research agreements designed to enhance regional employment. In the first, a research agreement appears successful because four start-up companies are developed within two years. Five years later, however, none of the start-up companies have survived and few, if any, inventions have been developed. The apparent short-term success of this collaborative agreement is illusory.

In the second example, a five-year research agreement fails to establish a single start-up company. The training of academic and industrial participants is so outstanding, however, that 15 years later, several participants are able to establish new companies. The apparent failure of this agreement is illusory.

At issue is whether short-term "return on investment" is an appropriate measure of success for the economic contributions of industry-university partnerships. Many state and federal leaders and some businessmen seem to accept return on investment as the principal criterion for measuring the success of these relationships. One observer strongly disagrees, however:

> *Investment to develop new business opportunities in the solution of social problems is much more like investment in long-range research and development than it is like investment in new manufacturing facilities. To say that such investments must be required to show a return in the long run is quite different from asking that its proponents demonstrate a highly probable return prior to the undertaking of the project* (Brooks 1984, p. 14).

Of particular concern is the focus on the university as the partner who must alter its behavior to meet the changing needs of the economy and to ensure the economic benefits of partnerships with industry. The ability of the industrial partner to absorb and use technological developments is even more crucial to achieving economic benefit from industry-university alliances (Chmura, Henton, and Melville 1988, p. 29; Feller 1988).

LESSONS FOR ACADEMIC, CORPORATE, AND GOVERNMENT LEADERS

To increase understanding of the variety of industry-university liaisons and their complexity, this monograph has described the emergence and expansion of alliances between business and higher education in the past decade, presented the ideological agendas and motivating factors behind this emergence, elaborated the variety of mechanisms and purposes of these liaisons, described the compatibility of relationships with industry for academic functions, and identified alternative approaches to assessment, including relevant criteria for measuring impact, effectiveness, and cost-effectiveness. This section examines implications of the literature review to assist academic, corporate, and government leaders in understanding existing industry-university arrangements and in preparing for future ones.

Generic Lessons

Many lessons transcend role and constituency, applying equally to leaders from government, industry, and academe. The five most important of these lessons are described in the following paragraphs.

Nature of science and innovation

Investment in science and in industry-university relationships designed to enhance it is better viewed as a matter of faith tempered by past evidence of success rather than as a rational cost-benefit economic decision. Any scientific or creative endeavor is to some extent a matter of chance; results are seldom guaranteed. Sometimes an industry-university research relationship may achieve desired results; sometimes it may not. Sometimes the results will justify the cost; sometimes they will not. Sometimes an innovative idea can be turned into a useful product; sometimes it cannot.

> *The plain fact is that no one knows how to stimulate innovation or whether, indeed, it is any more likely to be legislated into being than is any other creative act. Nor is it clear what interventions, if any, will enhance the growth of productive relations between parties still searching for specific expressions of interests that they hold generally in common* (Rosenzweig and Turlington 1982, p. 56).

The nature of the scientific enterprise argues against having unnecessarily high expectations for economic benefits from any industry-university alliance. It also argues strongly against

The key to any industry-university relationship is the match between capability and capacity of each participant on the one hand, and the goals and purposes of the liaison on the other.

using a narrow time framework for judging success or failure. Overreliance on application also may prove counterproductive: More than half of the recent discoveries in biomedical science resulted from basic research never intended for application (Comroe and Dripps 1976).

These lessons have meaning for the structure, focus, and goals of industry-university liaisons. Above all, they argue for developing reasonable expectations based on an understanding of how science and innovation occur.

Generalizability: A mistaken concept

In describing the purported success of their efforts, some advocates present guidelines for establishing successful industry-university relationships. To generate interest and enthusiasm, these presentations invariably encourage others to follow suit. Yet the evidence indicates that most, if not all, of the highly visible high-technology research agreements, such as those at Stanford University, Washington University, and Massachusetts Institute of Technology, are in their current locations for a reason: Not many others can do it (National Science Foundation 1982b, p. 25). As discussed later, developing successful industry-university arrangements is a function of capacity and talent as much as will and desire. For example, the popularity of biotechnology has led several states and universities to call for creation of biotechnology research centers to further economic development. The arguments are based on perceived benefit rather than on assessment of required resources. Without sufficient faculty, students, financial resources, and industrial interest, however, the effort cannot succeed (Carley 1988; Public Policy Center 1986).

Capacity and goals: The crucial match

The key to any industry-university relationship is the match between capability and capacity of each participant, on the one hand, and the goals and purposes of the liaison, on the other (Feller 1988; Friedman and Friedman 1985), requiring an objective assessment by both participants of relative strengths and weaknesses. Self-assessment is crucial both to understand the likelihood of success given current capabilities *and* to identify additional resources needed to make a specific arrangement work.

Deciding the relative importance of goals is also important. Industry-university agreements often are viewed as fulfilling multiple objectives. Which are most important? If resources are limited, which goals should be emphasized? Without deciding the relative importance of goals and using the decision to guide activities and allocate resources, a relationship may prove successful in ways valued little by participants while failing to meet more important objectives.

The end goal is for each participant (and sponsoring agency) to develop a relevant, reasonable, and well-understood rationale for participating in an alliance, including identification of a reasonable expectation for outcomes and appropriate criteria for judging impact and success.

Preserving distinctiveness and identity

The costs and benefits of industry-university relationships are most often viewed in the context of the relationship. Typical outcomes include economic benefits, patents and licenses, and the like. Beyond each relationship, however, lie the contributions made by academic institutions and businesses *as currently configured* to the general social and economic welfare. Although drastic changes to either type of institution may result in particular benefits, such changes may also lessen the ability to perform traditional functions well. If the capacity of universities to perform basic research, for example, is diminished, the long-term social and economic costs may exceed the benefits.

Recognition of the distinction between academe and industry is particularly important because many advocates of industry-university relationships obscure the fundamental differences in mission. Rather, business and higher education are viewed as two partners in the same enterprise (e.g., Lynton and Elman 1987; National Academy of Sciences 1983). The obfuscation of the distinction in missions and goals, which historically have not been identical (Finkle 1985; Knorr-Cetina 1981), may have negative consequences. Unlike industry, academe has maintained some distance from the changeability of the marketplace, a distance that has allowed colleges and universities to retain expertise and capacity in areas that might emerge again years later. As mentioned previously, the American economy would be substantially worse today if most colleges and universities responded 20 years ago to an oversupply of engineers by closing their schools of engineering. Making universities more responsive to the marketplace may result in desirable economic benefits, but negative consequences are also possible. Given the little evidence of substantial economic benefits from industry-university relationships to date, careful consideration of these broader costs and benefits is especially important:

> *Perhaps colleges and companies ought to stop short of taking each other's forms and functions, seeking instead to do what each can do best and cooperating with the other to complement their natural functions* (Aslanian and Brickell 1981, pp. 18–19).

Assessment: The forgotten factor

Virtually any analysis of industry-university relationships, whether descriptive or evaluative, would make decision making more effective. Rather than spending time addressing all potential threats to academic freedom, academic administrators would prefer to focus on a smaller number of demonstrably positive and negative factors. Advocates of industry-university alliances would benefit from knowing which relationships work best and should receive more resources. Given the extent of investment, the lack of evaluative or even descriptive data on these relationships is disheartening; continued failure to fund necessary research is unsupportable.

Lessons for State and Federal Governments

Two additional lessons exist for state and federal officials concerning the relationship between industry-university liaisons and economic development and the importance of governmental funding.

Economic development

Many governmental officials view academic institutions as requiring prodding to assist industry in reviving the national economy. The success of industry-university liaisons, however, depends equally on the ability of the corporate partner to absorb and use the technical innovations resulting from the liaison (Feller 1988). The assumption that alliances between business and higher education will make industry more innovative is probably unwise; more direct attention on industry is a better bet.

The role of industry-university research relationships in the production process is also often misunderstood. Even if potential products are identified in joint industry-university research projects, the manufacturing, production, and sales processes are clearly in the realm of the industrial partner. Again, the ability of the industrial partner to capitalize on the invention, not the ability of the collaborative research project to produce ideas, is crucial to achieving economic benefits.

In establishing programs to encourage industry-university partnerships, state officials try to target economic benefits to specific regions or to the state as a whole. The ability of a state or its regions to capture the economic benefits resulting from an alliance between business and higher education is not straightforward. For example, a particular liaison formed to benefit regional agriculture might instead produce a new chemical compound later found useful in treating cancer. If the state lacks prominent pharmaceutical or chemical companies, the economic benefits will go to states that have such industries (Public Policy Center 1986).

The federal government as funding agent

Although industrial funding of academic research has risen substantially, the vast majority of funding for academic research comes from the federal government (National Science Board 1987). Despite the appeal of industry-university relationships as vehicles for lessening the need for federal and state funds, the likelihood of such a change is minimal: "If the present level of academic research is to be maintained, the principal burden will fall on the public purse, federal and state" (Branscomb 1984, p. 46).

Providing funds for evaluating industry-university relationships also would be useful. The lack of evaluative data makes decisions about the utility of industry-university relationships difficult.

Lessons for Industry

Industrial leaders often are surprised that academic institutions do not operate in a "business-like fashion." Decisions relevant to industry-university alliances often are in the hands of faculty, not central administrators. Faculty may not respond to directives, instead pursuing lines of inquiry of personal interest. Extrinsic rewards found successful in industry, such as financial incentives, can be ineffective with faculty. As a group, faculty are motivated primarily by intrinsic rewards, such as intellectual stimulation, prestige, and respect of peers (McKeachie 1979, p. 20).

The cultural differences between industry and academe, of which faculty's motivation is only one, are substantial. Understanding these differences before negotiation is an important step in forming a successful liaison.

Lessons for Academe
Additional lessons for academic leaders interested in partnerships with industry focus on institutional policy, self-assessment, negotiation, and the nature of the relationship.

Institutional policy
Forming institutional policy for liaisons with industry can ensure the preservation of academic goals more effectively than leaving faculty and departments to strike their own bargains case by case. Success of a central policy depends on developing a clear mission statement before contract negotiations begin (Caldert 1983, p. 30).

Self-assessment
Understanding the capabilities and capacity of the academic institution before entering a relationship with industry is fundamental to success (Carley 1988, p. 28). Assessing relative risk is also important; using internal funds to support high-risk ventures with limited probabilities of return may not be advisable. Finally, awareness of motivation is crucial. Pursuing funds without a well-understood policy and set of goals and an understanding of the potential effect on academic activities increases the likelihood of negative consequences for the academic partner.

Negotiation
Academic administrators who have worked with industry previously and who understand the cultural differences between business and academe are more likely to negotiate agreements consistent with academic goals (Richter 1984, pp. 16–17). Also important is an understanding that highly visible potential conflicts, such as patent rights, are more easily dealt with contractually than are more subtle conflicts, such as undesirable changes in faculty behavior. The latter conflicts require a well-formulated policy and careful institutional placement of individuals working on the industry-university agreement.

Nature of the relationship
Coherent policies are necessary but not sufficient ingredients in ensuring compatible, successful industry-university relationships (Hansen 1983, p. 116). Some agreements may be incompatible

with the university's goals and values, regardless of policy. Short-term applied research projects with a focus on product development are one example (Geiger 1988; Rosenzweig and Turlington 1982, p. 8).

Some commentators argue that placement of an industry-university partnership whose compatibility with academic values is questionable in a peripheral organized research unit can protect academic values and goals (e.g., Baba 1985). The evidence suggests, however, that placement in an organized research unit supports academic goals and values only when the unit is committed to academic goals and values (Friedman and Friedman 1984, p. 30). In this light, placement of an industry-university partnership reflects a choice of values. If neither the goals of the agreement nor the values of the peripheral unit are strongly compatible with academic values, placing the agreement in a peripheral organization will not enhance academic values. If anything, such placement reinforces the separation of the peripheral organization from the college or university.

Finally, most industry-university relationships potentially contain costs and benefits for the college or university; the overall impact should be the concern of the academic administrator. Although the short-term benefits of some relationships with industry may be attractive, as these relationships move academic institutions toward application and product development, their relative advantage disappears:

> *In applied research and development, universities face strong competition from industry, government laboratories, and nonprofit research laboratories and have few comparative advantages in relation to these performers* (National Science Foundation 1982b, p. 21).

Above all, universities should retain the capacity to do what no other organization does as well: namely, to provide a broad liberal education for the populace, to train future professionals, and to combine basic research and instruction in the search for and dissemination of knowledge. Relationships with industry that enhance other goals without harming these basic functions may prove beneficial to a variety of audiences. The social costs of industry-university relationships that diminish the capacity of academic institutions to address fundamental, distinct missions may exceed the sum of their benefits, however.

REFERENCES

The Educational Resources Information Center (ERIC) Clearinghouse on Higher Education abstracts and indexes the current literature on higher education for inclusion in ERIC's data base and announcement in ERIC's monthly bibliographic journal, *Resources in Education* (RIE). Most of these publications are available through the ERIC Document Reproduction Service (EDRS). For publications cited in this bibliography that are available from EDRS, ordering number and price are included. Readers who wish to order a publication should write to the ERIC Document Reproduction Service, 3900 Wheeler Avenue, Alexandria, Virginia 22304. (Phone orders with VISA or MasterCard are taken at 800/227-ERIC or 703/823-0500.) When ordering, please specify the document (ED, HE, or SE) number. Documents are available as noted in microfiche (MF) and paper copy (PC). Because prices are subject to change, it is advisable to check the latest issue of *Resources in Education* for current cost based on the number of pages in the publication.

Aerospace Industries Association of America. 1983. "Meeting Technology and Manpower Needs through the Industry/University Interface: An Aerospace Industry Perspective." Washington, D.C.: Aerospace Research Center/Aerospace Technical Council. ED 239 848. 45 pp. MF–$1.07; PC–$5.79.

Alexander, Anne S. 1988. "Understanding the Philanthropic Partnership: Why Corporations Give." *Currents* 14 (3): 12–17.

Alpert, Daniel. 1985. "Performance and Paralysis: The Organizational Context for the American Research University." *Journal of Higher Education* 56 (3): 241–81.

American Association of Community and Junior Colleges. 1984. *Putting America Back to Work. The Kellogg Leadership Initiative: A Report and Guidebook*. Washington, D.C.: Author. ED 245 738. 66 pp. MF–$1.07; PC–$7.73.

Ashby, Eric. 1971. *Any Person, Any Study: An Essay on Higher Education in the United States*. New York: McGraw-Hill.

Ashford, Nicholas A. 1983. "A Framework for Examining the Effects of Industrial Funding on Academic Freedom and the Integrity of the University." *Science, Technology, and Human Values* 8 (2): 16–23.

Aslanian, Carol B., and Henry M. Brickell. Fall 1981. "On beyond Alliances? The New Reality for Companies and Colleges." *College Board Review* 121: 16–19 + .

Association of American Universities. 1986. *Trends in Technology Transfer at Universities*. Washington, D.C.: Author.

Astin, Alexander W., and Lewis C. Solomon. 1979. "Measuring Academic Quality: An Interim Report." *Change* 11 (6): 48–51.

Azaroff, Leonid V. 1982. "Industry-University Collaboration: How to Make It Work." *Research Management* 25 (3): 31–34.

Baaklini, Abdo I., John A. Worthley, and Jeffrey Apfel. 1979. "University and State Government Linkages." In *Linking Science and Technology to Public Policy: The Role of Universities*, edited by Abdo I. Baaklini. Albany: New York State Assembly and State University of New York–Albany.

Baba, Marietta. 1985. "University Innovation to Promote Economic Growth and University/Industry Relations." In *Promoting Economic Growth through Innovation: Proceedings of the Conference on Industrial Science and Technological Innovation*, edited by Pier Abetti, Christopher LeMaestre, and William Wallace. Albany: State University of New York–Albany.

Babco, Eleanor L. 1987. *Salaries of Scientists/Engineers and Technicians: A Summary of Salary Surveys*. 13th ed. Washington, D.C.: Scientific Manpower Commission. ED 292 625. 292 pp. MF–$1.07; PC not available EDRS.

Bach, Marilyn, and Ray Thornton. 1983. "Academic-Industrial Partnerships in Biomedical Research: Inevitability and Desirability." *Educational Record* 64 (2): 26–32.

Baldwin, Donald, and James Green. 1984–85. "University-Industry Relations: A Review of the Literature." *Journal of the Society of Research Administrators* 15 (4): 5–17.

Barthel, Susan V., and Julie A. Early. 1985. *The International Flow of Scientific and Technical Talent: Data, Policies, and Issues*. Washington, D.C.: Scientific Manpower Commission.

Bartlett, Joseph W., and James V. Siena. 1983–84. "Research and Development Limited Partnerships as a Device to Exploit University-Owned Technology." *Journal of College and University Law* 10 (4): 435–54.

Battenburg, Joseph R. 1980. "Forging Links between Industry and the Academic World." *Journal of the Society of Research Administrators* 12 (3): 5–12.

Bell, Daniel. 1973. *The Coming of the Post-industrial Society: A Venture in Social Forecasting*. New York: Basic Books.

———. 1979. "Communications Technology—For Better or for Worse." *Harvard Business Review* 57 (3): 20 + .

Bernstein, Melvin H. 1986. *Higher Education and the State: New Linkages for Economic Development*. Washington, D.C.: National Institute for Work and Learning. ED 274 303. 46 pp. MF–$1.07; PC–$5.79.

Blackburn, Robert T., and Paul E. Lingenfelter. 1973. *Assessing Quality in Doctoral Programs: Criteria and Correlates of Excellence*. Ann Arbor: Univ. of Michigan. ED 078 728. 54 pp. MF–$1.07; PC–$7.73.

Blumenthal, David, Sherrie Epstein, and James Maxwell. 1986. "Commercializing University Research: Lessons from the Experience of the Wisconsin Alumni Research Fund." *New England Journal of Medicine* 314 (25): 1621–26.

Blumenthal, David, Michael Gluck, Karen Louis, Michael Stoto, and David Wise. 1986. "University-Industry Research Relationships in Biotechnology: Implications for the University." *Science* 232 (4756): 1361–66.

Bok, Derek. 1982. *Beyond the Ivory Tower*. Cambridge, Mass.: Harvard Univ. Press.

Botkin, James, Dan Dimancescu, and Ray Strata. 1982. *Global Stakes: The Future of High Technology in America*. Cambridge, Mass.: Ballinger.

Bowen, Howard. 1977. *Investment in Learning: The Individual and Social Value of American Higher Education*. San Francisco: Jossey-Bass.

Bowen, Howard R., and Jack H. Schuster. 1986. *American Professors: A National Resource Imperiled*. New York: Oxford Univ. Press.

Boyer, Ernest L. 1987. *College: The Undergraduate Experience in America*. New York: Harper & Row.

Boyle, M. Ross. 1983. "College/Business Marriage: 'Sensible' Response to Hard Times." *Community and Junior College Journal* 54 (3): 15–17.

Branscomb, Lewis M. 1984. "America's Rising Research Alliance." *American Education* 20 (6): 43–46.

Brazziel, William F. 1981a. "College-Corporate Partnerships in Higher Education." *Educational Record* 62 (2): 50–53.

———. 1981b. *College/Corporate Partnerships: Studies in Cooperative Efforts in Education and Staff Development*. Washington, D.C.: National Institute of Education. ED 202 425. 14 pp. MF–$1.07; PC–$3.85.

Broad, William J. 1982. "Pajaro Dunes: The Search for Consensus." *Science* 216 (4542): 155.

Broce, Thomas E. 1986. *Fund Raising: The Guide to Raising Money from Private Sources*. 2d rev. ed. Norman: Univ. of Oklahoma Press.

Brooks, Harvey. 1984. "Seeking Equity and Efficiency: Public and Private Roles." In *Public-Private Partnership: New Opportunities for Meeting Social Needs*, edited by H. Brooks, L. Liebman, and C. Schelling. Cambridge, Mass.: Ballinger.

Buchbinder, Howard, and Janice Newson. 1985. "Corporate-University Linkages and the Scientific-Technical Revolution." *Interchange* 16 (3): 37–53.

Burdette, Melinda J. 1988. "Choose Your Partnership: A Sampling of Campus-Corporate Pairings." *Currents* 14 (3): 18–25.

Burger, Lynn T. 1984. "The Progress of Partners." *Community and Junior College Journal* 55 (3): 36–39.

Bush, Vannevar. 1945. *Science: The Endless Frontier*. Washington, D.C.: U.S. Government Printing Office.

Business–Higher Education Forum. 1984. *Corporate and Campus Cooperation: An Action Agenda*. Washington, D.C.: Author.

———. 1988a. *Beyond the Rhetoric: Evaluating University-Industry Cooperation in Research and Technology Exchange*. Vol. 1, The Case. Washington, D.C.: Author.

———. 1988b. *Beyond the Rhetoric: Evaluating University-Industry Cooperation in Research and Technology Exchange*. Vol. 2, A Handbook. Washington, D.C.: Author.

"Business and Universities: A New Partnership." 20 December 1982. *Business Week* (2770): 58–62.

Caffrey, John, and Herbert Isaacs. 1971. *Estimating the Impact of a College or University on the Local Economy*. Washington, D.C.: American Council on Education. ED 252 100. 83 pp. MF–$1.07; PC–$10.03.

Caldert, Charles C. 1983. "Industry Investment in University Research." *Science, Technology, and Human Values* 8 (2): 24–32.

California Postsecondary Education Commission. 1984. *The Wealth of Knowledge*. Sacramento: Author. ED 247 833. 42 pp. MF–$1.07; PC–$5.79.

Carley, David. 1988. "Enter the Entrepreneur: Engaging in Large-Scale Business Development." *Currents* 14 (3): 26–33.

Carnegie Commission on Higher Education. 1976. *A Classification of Institutions of Higher Education*. Berkeley, Cal.: Author.

Charner, Ivan, and Catherine Rolzinski. 1987. "New Directions for Responding to a Changing Economy." In *Responding to the Educational Needs of Today's Workforce*, edited by Ivan Charner and Catherine Rolzinski. San Francisco: Jossey-Bass.

Chmura, Thomas J. 1987. "The Higher Education–Economic Development Connection: Emerging Roles for Colleges and Universities." *Economic Development Commentary* 11 (3): 1–7.

Chmura, Thomas, Douglas Henton, and John Melville. 1987. *Corporate Education and Training: Investing in a Competitive Future*. Menlo Park, Cal.: SRI International.

———. 1988. *California's Higher Education System: Adding Economic Competitiveness to the Higher Education Agenda*. Menlo Park, Cal.: SRI International.

Choate, Pat. 1986. "Business and Higher Education: Imperative to Adapt." In *Issues in Higher Education and Economic Development*. Washington, D.C.: American Association of State Colleges and Universities.

Clark, Burton R. 1987. *The Academic Life*. New York: Carnegie Foundation.

Clark, Mary J., Rodney T. Hartnett, and Leonard L. Baird. 1976. *Assessing Dimensions of Quality in Doctoral Education: A Tech-*

nical Report of a National Study in Three Fields. Princeton, N.J.:
Educational Testing Service. ED 173 144. 427 pp. MF–$1.07; PC–
$37.46.

Clark, Richard J. 1984. "Factors Influencing Success in a School-
University-Industry Partnership for Teacher Education." Report on
the Math/Science/Technology Education Project. ED 258 955. 5 pp.
MF–$1.07; PC–$3.85.

Cole, Charles C., Jr. 1982. *Improving Instruction: Issues and Alter-
natives for Higher Education*. AAHE-ERIC Higher Education
Report No. 4. Washington, D.C.: American Association for Higher
Education.

Comroe, Julius H., Jr., and Robert D. Dripps. 1976. "Scientific
Basis for the Support of Biomedical Science." *Science* 192 (4235):
105–11.

Corporation for Penn State. 1986. *Ben Franklin Partnership: The
Advanced Technology Center of Central and Northern Pennsylvania, 1985–86 Annual Report*. University Park, Pa.: Author.

Council for Financial Aid to Education. 1988. *Voluntary Support of
Education: 1986–1987*. New York: Author. HE 021 961. 90 pp.
MF–$1.07; PC–$10.03.

Craig, Robert L., and Christine J. Evers. 1981. "Employers as Edu-
cators: The 'Shadow Education System.' " In *Business and Higher
Education: Toward New Alliances*, edited by Gerald G. Gold. New
Directions for Experiential Learning No. 13. San Francisco:
Jossey-Bass.

Cross, K. Patricia. 1981. "New Frontiers for Higher Education:
Business and the Professions." In *Partnerships with Business and
the Professions*. 1981 Current Issues in Higher Education No. 3.
Washington, D.C.: American Association of Higher Education.

Crosson, Patricia. 1986. "Encouraging Faculty Involvement in University Economic Development Programs." In *Issues in Higher
Education and Economic Development*. Washington, D.C.: American Association of State Colleges and Universities.

Culliton, Barbara J. 1981. "Biomedical Research Enters the Marketplace." *New England Journal of Medicine* 304 (2): 1195–1201.

David, Edward E., Jr. 1982. "Supporting Research with a Commercial Mission." *Change* 14 (6): 26–29.

Day, Philip R. 1985. *In Search of Community College Partnerships*.
Keeping America Working Series No. 2. Washington, D.C.: American Association of Community and Junior Colleges. ED 258 626.
67 pp. MF–$1.07; PC–$7.73.

Declerq, Guido V. October 1979. "Technology Transfer from Campus
to Industry." *International Journal of Institutional Management in
Higher Education* 3: 237–52.

Derber, Charles. 1987. "Worker Education for a Changing Economy:

New Labor-Academic Partnerships." In *Responding to the Educational Needs of Today's Workforce*, edited by Ivan Charner and Catherine Rolzinski. San Francisco: Jossey-Bass.

Dickson, David. 1984. *The New Politics of Science*. New York: Pantheon Books.

Dimancescu, Dan, and James Botkin. 1986. *The New Alliance: America's R&D Consortia*. Cambridge, Mass.: Ballinger.

Doigan, Paul. 1984a. "ASEE Survey of Engineering Faculty and Graduate Students, Fall 1983." *Engineering Education* 75 (1): 50–55.

———. 1984b. *Fall 1983 ASEE Survey of Engineering Faculty and Graduate Students*. Washington, D.C.: Association of Engineering Education.

Doigan, Paul, and Mark Gilkeson. 1986. "ASEE Survey of Engineering Faculty and Graduate Students, Fall 1985." *Engineering Education* 77 (1): 51–57.

Douglas, Joel M., ed. September/October 1984. "Do Academic/Corporate Partnerships Pose New Threats to Faculty Employment in Institutions of Higher Education?" *Newsletter of the National Center for the Study of Collective Bargaining in Higher Education and the Professions* 4: 1–6. ED 250 995. 8 pp. MF–$1.07; PC–$3.85.

Dowling, Michael. 1987. "Science and Technology Policy: Present Developments and Future Trends." In *Promoting High-Technology Industry*, edited by Jurgen Schmandt and Robert Wilson. Boulder, Colo.: Westview Press.

Dressel, Paul. 1987. "Mission, Organization, and Leadership." *Journal of Higher Education* 58 (1): 101–9.

Drew, David E. 1985. *Strengthening Academic Science*. New York: Praeger.

Duscha, Steve. 1984. "Retooling for Productivity." *Community and Junior College Journal* 55 (3): 40–42.

Ellison, Nolen M. 1983. "BICCC: An Important Community College Initiative." Paper presented at the Business Industry Coalition seminar sponsored by the Kansas Association of Community Colleges, January, Topeka, Kansas. ED 227 891. 14 pp. MF–$1.07; PC–$3.85.

Eurich, Nell P. 1985. *Corporate Classrooms: The Learning Business*. Princeton, N.J.: Carnegie Foundation for the Advancement of Teaching. ED 264 785. 127 pp. MF–$1.07; PC not available EDRS.

Fairweather, James S. 1988. "Reputational Quality of Academic Programs: The Institutional Halo." *Research in Higher Education* 28 (4): 345–56.

———. n.d. "Academic Research and Instruction: The Industrial Connection." *Journal of Higher Education*. In press.

Feller, Irwin. 1986. "An Evolutionary Perspective on Emerging University-Corporate-State Government Research and Development Relationships." Paper presented at a meeting of the Association for Public Policy Analysis and Management, October, Austin, Texas.

———. 1988. "University-Industry Research and Development Relationships." Paper prepared for the Woodlands Center for Growth Studies Conference, November, Houston, Texas.

Finkle, Bryan S. 1985. "Industry-University: Partners in Myth and Reality." *American Journal of Pharmaceutical Education* 49 (4): 378–80.

Foster, Badi G. 1986. "The Relationship between Corporate and Higher Education." *Journal of Cooperative Education* 22 (2): 48–53.

Fowler, Donald. 1982–83. "University-Industry Research Relationships: The Research Agreement." *Journal of College and University Law* 9 (4): 515–32.

———. 1984. "University-Industry Research Relationships." *Research Management* 27 (1): 35–41.

Fox, Shirley. 1985. *New PIC/Postsecondary Partnerships: How Postsecondary Institutions and Private Industry Councils Are Working Together to Boost Economic Development and Put People Back to Work.* Washington, D.C.: National Institute for Work and Learning. ED 269 617. 31 pp. MF–$1.07; PC–$5.79.

Friedman, Robert S., and Renee C. Friedman. 1984. "Managing the Organized Research Unit." *Educational Record* 65 (1): 27–30.

———. 1985. "Organized Research Units in Academe Revisited." In *Managing High Technology: An Interdisciplinary Perspective*, edited by Brian W. Mar, William T. Newell, and Borje O. Saxberg. New York: Elsevier Science Publishing Company.

Fusfeld, Herbert I. 1983. "Overview of University-Industry Research Interactions." In *Partners in the Research Enterprise: University-Corporate Relations in Science and Technology*, edited by Thomas W. Langfitt, Sheldon Hackney, Alfred P. Fishman, and Albert V. Glowasky. Philadelphia: Univ. of Pennsylvania Press.

Fusfeld, Herbert I., and Carmela S. Haklisch. 1987. "Collaborative Industrial Research in the U.S." *Technovation* 5 (4): 305–16.

Gavert, Roy. 1983. "Business and Academe—An Emerging Partnership." *Change* 15 (3): 23–28.

Geiger, Roger L. 1986. *To Advance Knowledge: The Growth of American Research Universities, 1900–1940.* New York: Oxford Univ. Press.

———. 1988. "Milking the Sacred Cow: Research and the Quest for Useful Knowledge in the American University since 1920." *Science, Technology, and Human Values* 13 (3–4): 322–48.

Giamatti, A. Bartlett. 1983. "Free Market and Free Inquiry: The

University, Industry, and Cooperative Research." In *Partners in the Research Enterprise: University-Corporate Relations in Science and Technology*, edited by Thomas W. Langfitt, Sheldon Hackney, Alfred P. Fishman, and Albert V. Glowasky. Philadelphia: Univ. of Pennsylvania Press.

Gilley, J. Wade. 1986. "Higher Education and Economic Development." In *Issues in Higher Education and Economic Development*. Washington, D.C.: American Association of State Colleges and Universities.

Gold, Gerald G. 1981. "Toward Business–Higher Education Alliances." In *Business and Higher Education: Toward New Alliances*, edited by Gerald G. Gold. New Directions for Experiential Learning No. 13. San Francisco: Jossey-Bass.

Gold, Gerald G., and Ivan Charner. 1986. *Higher Education Partnerships*. Washington, D.C.: National Institute for Work and Learning. ED 281 419. 40 pp. MF–$1.07; PC–$5.79.

Government-University-Industry Research Roundtable. 1986. *New Alliances and Partnerships in American Science and Engineering*. Washington, D.C.: National Academy Press. SE 049 725. 132 pp. MF–$1.07; PC–$14.01.

Government-University-Industry Research Roundtable and the Industrial Research Institute. 1988. *Simplified and Standardized Model Agreements for University-Industry Cooperative Research*. Washington, D.C.: National Academy Press. SE 049 729. 11 pp. MF–$1.07; PC–$3.85.

Green, Joan. 1985. "For Foothill College: Corporate Partnerships Are Win-Win Situations." *AGB Reports* 27 (6): 30–32.

Haddad, Jerrier A. 1986. "New Factors in the Relationship between Engineering Education and Research." In *The New Engineering Research Centers: Purposes, Goals, and Expectations*. Washington, D.C.: National Academy Press.

Haller, H. 1984. "Examples of University-Industry (Government) Collaborations." Unpublished manuscript. Office of the Vice President for Research and Advanced Studies, Cornell Univ.

Hambrick, Ralph S., Jr., and Gerald S. Swanson. 1979. "The Mobilization of Expertise: The Problems of Managing Applied Research in a University." In *Linking Science and Technology to Public Policy: The Role of Universities*, edited by Abdo I. Baaklini. Albany: New York State Assembly and State University of New York–Albany.

Hansen, Arthur G. 1983. "The Industrial-Education Partnership: The Promise and the Problems." *Technological Horizons in Education* 11 (2): 113–16.

Harris, James. 1988. "An Assessment of Factors Related to Successful Fund Raising at Public, Doctorate-Granting Universities." D.Ed. dissertation, Pennsylvania State Univ.

Hatsopoulos, George N., Paul R. Krugman, and Lawrence H. Summers. 1988. "U.S. Competitiveness: Beyond the Trade Deficit." *Science* 241 (4863): 299–307.

Hersh, Richard. 1983. "Education and the Corporate Connection." *Educational Horizons* 62 (1): 5–8.

Hines, Edward R. 1987. *Appropriations: State Tax Funds for Operating Expenses of Higher Education, 1986–87.* Washington, D.C.: National Association of State Universities and Land-Grant Colleges. ED 283 473. 32 pp. MF–$1.07; PC–$5.79.

Holmstrom, Engin I., and Janice Petrovich. 1985. *Engineering Programs in Emerging Areas, 1983–84.* Higher Education Panel Report No. 64. Washington, D.C.: American Council on Education. ED 265 776. 53 pp. MF–$1.07; PC–$7.73.

Houle, Cyril. 1980. *Continuing Learning in the Professions.* San Francisco: Jossey-Bass.

Hurwitz, Sol. 1982. "Civic Partners: Business and Liberal Education." *Liberal Education* 68 (4): 329–37.

Hutchins, Robert M. 1962. *The Higher Learning in America.* 2d ed. New Haven, Conn.: Yale Univ. Press.

Hutt, Peter B. 1983. "University/Corporate Research Agreements." *Technology in Society* 5 (2): 107–18.

Ikenberry, Stanley O., and Renee C. Friedman. 1972. *Beyond Academic Departments: The Story of Institutions and Centers.* San Francisco: Jossey-Bass.

Johnson, Elmima C., and Louis G. Tornatzky. 1981. "Academia and Industrial Innovation." In *Business and Higher Education: Toward New Alliances*, edited by Gerald G. Gold. New Directions for Experiential Learning No. 13. San Francisco: Jossey-Bass.

———. 1984. *Cooperative Science: A National Study of University and Industry Researchers.* Washington, D.C.: National Science Foundation. ED 293 692. 42 pp. MF–$1.07; PC–$5.79.

Johnson, Lynn G. 1984. *The High-Technology Connection: Academic/Industrial Cooperation for Economic Growth.* ASHE-ERIC Higher Education Report No. 6. Washington, D.C.: Association for the Study of Higher Education. ED 255 130. 129 pp. MF–$1.07; PC–$14.01.

Johnston, Robert F., and Christopher G. Edwards. 1987. *Entrepreneurial Science: New Links between Corporations, Universities, and Government.* Westport, Conn.: Greenwood Press.

Jones, Lyle V., Gardner Lindzey, and Porter E. Coggeshall, eds. 1982a. *An Assessment of Research-Doctorate Programs in the United States: Engineering.* Washington, D.C.: National Academy Press. ED 243 673. 200 pp. MF–$1.07; PC not available EDRS.

———. 1982b. *An Assessment of Research-Doctorate Programs in the United States: Humanities.* Washington, D.C.: National Academy Press. ED 243 336. 248 pp. MF–$1.07; PC–$22.60.

————. 1982c. *An Assessment of Research-Doctorate Programs in the United States: Mathematics and Physical Sciences*. Washington, D.C.: National Academy Press. ED 243 675. 250 pp. MF–$1.07; PC–$22.60.

————. 1982d. *An Assessment of Research-Doctorate Programs in the United States: Social and Behavioral Sciences*. Washington, D.C.: National Academy Press. ED 243 337. 254 pp. MF–$1.07; PC–$24.54.

Keller, George. 1983. *Academic Strategy*. Baltimore: Johns Hopkins Univ. Press.

Kenney, Martin. 1986. *Biotechnology: The University-Industrial Complex*. New Haven, Conn.: Yale Univ. Press.

Knorr-Cetina, Karin D. 1981. *The Manufacture of Knowledge: An Essay on the Constructivist and Contextual Nature of Science*. Oxford: Pergamon Press.

Kreps, Juanita. 1986. "Maintaining the Nation's Competitiveness." In *Issues in Higher Education and Economic Development*. Washington, D.C.: American Association of State Colleges and Universities.

Larsen, Judith, and Rolf Wigand. 1987. "Industry-University Technology Transfer in Microelectronics." *Policy Studies Review* 6 (3): 584–95.

Lawrence, Paul R., and Jay W. Lorsch. 1967. *Organizations and Environment*. Boston: Harvard Univ. Press.

Levin, Richard, Wesley Cohen, and David Mowery. 1985. "R&D Appropriability, Opportunity Market Structure: New Evidence on Some Schumpeterian Hypotheses." *American Economic Review* 75 (2): 20–24.

Link, Albert, and George Tassey. 1987. *Strategies for Technology-Based Competition*. Lexington, Mass.: Lexington Books.

Linnell, Robert H., ed. 1982. *Dollars and Scholars: An Inquiry into the Impact of Faculty Income upon the Function and Future of the Academy*. Los Angeles: Univ. of Southern California Press.

Logan, Lawrence B., and Jacob O. Stampen. 1985. "Smoke Stack Meets Ivory Tower: Collaborations with Local Industry." *Educational Record* 66 (2): 26–29.

Long, Wesley, and Irwin Feller. 1972. "State Support for Research and Development: An Uncertain Path to Economic Growth." *Land Economics* 48 (3): 220–27.

Low, George M. 1983. "The Organization of Industrial Relationships in Universities." In *Partners in the Research Enterprise: University-Corporate Relations in Science and Technology*, edited by Thomas W. Langfitt, Sheldon Hackney, Alfred P. Fishman, and Albert V. Glowasky. Philadelphia: Univ. of Pennsylvania Press.

Lyall, Katherine C., and M. Ramona Montoya. 1981. *Economic Impact of the Johns Hopkins Institutions on Baltimore City, 1980*. Baltimore: Johns Hopkins Univ.

Lynton, Ernest A. 1981. "A Role for Colleges in Corporate Training and Development." In *Partnerships with Business and the Professions*. Current Issues in Higher Education No. 3. Washington, D.C.: American Association for Higher Education.

Lynton, Ernest A., and Sandra E. Elman. 1987. *New Priorities for the University*. San Francisco: Jossey-Bass.

Lyon, Richard E., Jr. 1982. "A Bridge Reconnecting Universities and Industry through Basic Research." In *The Research System in the 1980s: Public Policy Issues*, edited by John M. Longsdon. Philadelphia: Franklin Institute Press.

McKeachie, Wilbert J. 1979. "Perspectives from Psychology: Financial Incentives Are Ineffective for Faculty." In *Academic Rewards in Higher Education*, edited by Darrell Lewis and William Becker, Jr. Cambridge, Mass.: Ballinger.

MacKenzie, Ian, and Roderick Rhys Jones. 1985. *Universities and Industry: New Opportunities for Collaboration with UK Universities and Polytechnics*. Special Report No. 213. London: Economist Intelligence Unit.

McMullen, Harold G. 1984. "Community College Business and Industry Educational Partnership: An Essential Industrial Development Linkage." Position paper from Lord Fairfax Community College. ED 244 709. 10 pp. MF–$1.07; PC–$3.85.

Mai, Klaus L. 1984. "University and Industry—A Productive Relationship." *American Education* 20 (6): 2–4.

Matthews, Jana B., and Rolf Norgaard. 1984. *Managing the Partnership between Higher Education and Industry*. Boulder, Colo.: National Center for Higher Education Management Systems. ED 246 823. 253 pp. MF–$1.07; PC–$24.54.

Maxfield, Betty D. 1982. *Science, Engineering, and Humanities Doctorates in the United States: 1981 Profile*. Washington, D.C.: National Academy Press.

Michel, Jean. 1985. "Higher Education and Industry: Towards a New Partnership for Improving Engineering Education." *European Journal of Engineering Education* 10 (2): 149–54.

Moser, Katherine. 1986. "Business-Industry Linkages with Postsecondary Institutions: Implications for Building Successful Partnerships." *Lifelong Learning* 9 (7): 4–5 + .

Muller, Steven. 1982. "Basic Research on the Campus: A University View." In *The Research System in the 1980s: Public Policy Issues*, edited by John M. Longsdon. Philadelphia: Franklin Institute Press.

National Academy of Engineering. 1983. *Guidelines for Engineering Research Centers*. Washington, D.C.: Author.

———. 1988. *The Technological Dimensions of International Competitiveness*. Washington, D.C.: Author.

National Academy of Sciences. 1983. *Strengthening the Government-*

University Partnership in Science. Washington, D.C.: National Academy Press. ED 283 887. 248 pp. MF–$1.07; PC not available EDRS.

National Research Council. 1985a. *Engineering Education and Practice in the United States: Continuing Education of Engineers*. Washington, D.C.: National Academy Press.

———. 1985b. *Engineering Education and Practice in the United States: Foundations of Our Techno-Economic Future*. Washington, D.C.: National Academy Press.

———. 1985c. *Information and Technology Exchange among Engineering Research Centers and Industry: Report of a Workshop*. Washington, D.C.: National Academy Press.

———. 1985d. *Support Organizations for the Engineering Community*. Washington, D.C.: National Academy Press. SE 049 212. 67 pp. MF–$1.07; PC–$7.73.

National Science Board. 1985. *Science Indicators: The 1985 Report*. Washington, D.C.: U. S. Government Printing Office. ED 266 043. 333 pp. MF–$1.07; PC–$30.70.

———. 1986. *Undergraduate Science, Mathematics, and Engineering Education*. Washington, D.C.: Author. ED 272 398. 67 pp. MF–$1.07; PC–$7.73.

———. 1987. *Science and Engineering Indicators, 1987*. Washington, D.C.: Author. SE 049 141. 353 pp. MF–$1.07; PC–$32.64.

National Science Foundation. 1981. *Science and Engineering Employment, 1970–1980*. Washington, D.C.: Author. ED 210 179. 26 pp. MF–$1.07; PC–$5.79.

———. 1982a. *Science and Engineering Personnel: A National Overview*. Washington, D.C.: Author. ED 225 848. 77 pp. MF–$1.07; PC–$10.03.

———. 1982b. *University-Industry Research Relationships: Myths, Realities, and Potentials*. Fourteenth annual report of the National Science Board. Washington, D.C.: Author. ED 230 115. 39 pp. MF–$1.07; PC–$5.79.

———. 1984a. *Academic Science/Engineering: R&D Funds, Fiscal Year 1982*. Washington, D.C.: Author. ED 244 838. 155 pp. MF–$1.07; PC–$16.36.

———. 1984b. *Science and Engineering Personnel: A National Overview*. Washington, D.C.: Author. ED 257 646. 239 pp. MF–$1.07; PC–$22.60.

———. 1985a. *Academic Science/Engineering: Graduate Enrollment and Support, Fall 1983*. Washington, D.C.: Author. ED 256 606. 300 pp. MF–$1.07; PC–$26.48.

———. 1985b. *Academic Science/Engineering: Scientists and Engineers, January 1984*. Washington, D.C.: Author. ED 257 650. 116 pp. MF–$1.07; PC–$12.07.

————. 1985c. *Characteristics of Doctoral Scientists and Engineers in the United States, 1983*. Washington, D.C.: Author. ED 256 605. 115 pp. MF–$1.07; PC–$12.07.

————. 1985d. "Early Release of Summary Statistics in Academic Science/Engineering Resources." Washington, D.C.: Author.

National Science Foundation and U.S. Department of Education. 1980. *Science and Engineering Education for the 1980s and Beyond*. Washington, D.C.: U.S. Government Printing Office. ED 193 092. 228 pp. MF–$1.07; PC–$22.60.

Nelson, Richard, ed. 1982. *Government and Technical Progress*. New York: Pergamon Press.

————. 1986. "Institutions Supporting Technical Advance in Industry." *American Economic Review* 76 (2): 186–90.

Noble, David F. 1977. *America by Design: Science, Technology, and the Rise of Corporate Capitalism*. New York: Oxford Univ. Press.

Noble, David F., and Nancy E. Pfund. 1980. "The Plastic Tower: Business Goes Back to College." *Nation* 231 (8): 233+.

Nowlen, Philip N., and Milton R. Stern. 1981. "Partnerships in Continuing Education for Professionals." In *Partnerships with Business and the Professions*. Current Issues in Higher Education No. 3. Washington, D.C.: American Association for Higher Education. ED 213 325. 27 pp. MF–$1.07; PC–$5.79.

Office of Science and Technology Policy. 1986. *A Renewed Partnership: Report of the White House Science Council Panel on the Health of U.S. Colleges and Universities*. Washington, D.C.: Author. ED 268 945. 57 pp. MF–$1.07; PC–$7.73.

Parnell, Dale. 1986. "Shaping the Environment." Paper presented at the 66th Annual Convention of the American Association of Community and Junior Colleges, April, Orlando, Florida. ED 269 070. 10 pp. MF–$1.07; PC–$3.85.

Parnell, Dale, and Roger Yarrington. 1982. *Proven Partners: Business, Labor, and Community Colleges*. Washington, D.C.: American Association of Community and Junior Colleges. ED 214 582. 59 pp. MF–$1.07; PC–$7.73.

Peters, Lois, and Herbert Fusfeld. 1983. "Current U.S. University/Industry Research Connections." In *University-Industry Research Relationships: Selected Studies*. Washington, D.C.: National Science Foundation.

Peterson, Ivars. 1983. "Academic Questions: Campus and Company Partnerships." *Science News* 123 (5): 76–77.

Ping, Charles J. 1981. "Bigger Stake for Business in Higher Education." *Harvard Business Review* 59 (5): 122–29.

Powers, David R., Mary F. Powers, Frederick Betz, and Carol B. Aslanian. 1988. *Higher Education in Partnership with Industry: Opportunities for Training, Research, and Economic Development*. San Francisco: Jossey-Bass.

Praeger, Denis J., and Gilbert S. Omenn. 1980. "Research, Innovation, and University-Industry Linkages." *Science* 207 (4429): 379–84.

Price, Don K. 1965. *The Scientific Estate*. Cambridge, Mass.: Belknap Press of Harvard Univ. Press.

Public Policy Center, SRI International. 1986. *The Higher Education–Economic Development Connection: Emerging Roles for Public Colleges and Universities in a Changing Economy*. Washington, D.C.: American Association of State Colleges and Universities.

Reams, Bernard, Jr. 1986. *University-Industry Research Partnerships*. Westport, Conn.: Quorum Books.

Richter, Maurice N. 1984. "Industrial Funding of Faculty Research." Paper presented at the Society for Social Studies of Science, November, Ghent, Belgium.

Rinehart, Richard L. 1982. "Industry-College Cooperation: New Components, Barriers, and Strategies." Paper presented at the annual convention of the American Association of Community and Junior Colleges, 4–7 April, St. Louis, Missouri. ED 215 739. 16 pp. MF–$1.07; PC–$3.85.

Roose, Kenneth D., and Charles J. Anderson. 1970. *A Rating of Graduate Programs*. Washington, D.C.: American Council on Education.

Rosenzweig, Robert M., and Barbara Turlington. 1982. *The Research Universities and Their Patrons*. Berkeley: Univ. of California Press.

Samuels, Frank. 1985. "A Creative Partnership for the Community College and Business and Industry in Occupational Upgrading and Retraining." Paper presented at the annual meeting of the Commission on Institutions of Higher Education, March, Chicago, Illinois. ED 255 277. 25 pp. MF–$1.07; PC–$3.85.

Schmitt, Roland W. 1986. "Engineering Research and International Competitiveness." In *The New Engineering Research Centers: Purposes, Goals, and Expectations*. Washington, D.C.: National Academy Press.

Schuh, G. Edward. Second Quarter 1986. "Revitalizing Land-Grant Universities: It's Time to Regain Relevance." *Choices*: 6–10.

Sheppard, Ronald J. 1986. "Research and Development and the Role of the Urban University in Strategic Economic Development Planning." Paper presented at the International Urban Universities Conference, September, Winnipeg, Manitoba. ED 277 799. 13 pp. MF–$1.07; PC–$3.85.

Skocpol, Theda. 1985. "Bringing the State Back In: Strategy Analysis of Current Research." In *Bringing the State Back In*, edited by Peter B. Evans, Dietrich Rueschmyer, and Theda Skocpol. Cambridge: Cambridge Univ. Press.

Slaughter, Sheila. n.d. *The Higher Learning and High Technology:*

Dynamics of Higher Education Policy Formation. Albany: State
Univ. of New York Press. In press.

Smith, Hayden W. 1988. "Business Sense: The Underpinnings of
Today's Corporate-Campus Relationships." *Currents* 14 (3): 6–11.

Smith, Peter. 1986. "A Policy Environment for Human Capital Development." In *Issues in Higher Education and Economic Development*. Washington, D.C.: American Association of State Colleges and Universities.

Stankiewicz, Rikard. 1986. *Academics and Entrepreneurs: Developing
University-Industry Relations*. London: Frances Pinter.

Stark, Joan S., Malcolm A. Lowther, and Bonnie M.K. Hagerty.
1986. *Responsive Professional Education: Balancing Outcomes and
Opportunities*. ASHE-ERIC Higher Education Report No. 3. Washington, D.C.: Association for the Study of Higher Education. ED
273 229. 144 pp. MF–$1.07; PC–$14.01.

Stauffer, Thomas M. 1979. "Expanding Business–Higher Education
Cooperation on Research and Development." *Journal of the Society
of Research Administrators* 11 (1): 41–46.

———. 1986. "The Responsibilities of Public Universities for
Economic Development." In *Issues in Higher Education and
Economic Development*. Washington, D.C.: American Association
of State Colleges and Universities.

Stern, Joyce D., and Marjorie O. Chandler, eds. 1987. *The Condition
of Education*. Washington, D.C.: National Center for Education
Statistics. ED 284 371. 252 pp. MF–$1.07; PC–$24.54.

Study Group on the Conditions of Excellence in American Higher
Education. 1984. *Involvement in Learning: Realizing the Potential
of American Higher Education*. Washington, D.C.: U.S. Department of Education. ED 246 833. 127 pp. MF–$1.07; PC–$14.01.

Swanson, David H. 1986. "Transferring Technologies to Industry."
In *Issues in Higher Education and Economic Development*. Washington, D.C.: American Association of State Colleges and Universities.

Tatel, David S., and R. Guthrie. 1983. "The Legal Ins and Outs of
University-Industry Collaboration." *Educational Record* 64 (2):
19–25.

Teich, Albert H. 1982. "Research Centers and Nonfaculty Researchers." In *Research in the Age of the Steady-State University*, edited
by Don I. Phillips and Benjamin S.P. Shen. Boulder, Colo.:
Westview Press.

Theede, Marcy P. 1985. "Improving Education through Greater
Partnerships with Business and Industry." Paper presented at the
annual conference of the National Council of States on Inservice
Education, November, Denver, Colorado. ED 273 232. 12 pp. MF–
$1.07; PC–$3.85.

Tuckman, Howard. 1979. "The Academic Reward Structure in American Higher Education." In *Academic Rewards in Higher Education*, edited by Darrell Lewis and William Becker, Jr. Cambridge, Mass.: Ballinger.

U.S. Department of Commerce. 1980. *Cooperative R&D Programs to Stimulate Industrial Innovation in Selected Countries*. Washington, D.C.: Author.

U.S. General Accounting Office. 1988. *Engineering Research Centers: NSF Program Management and Industry Sponsorship*. Washington, D.C.: Author. SE 049 708. 80 pp. MF–$1.07; PC–$10.03.

U.S. Office of Technology Assessment. 1984. *Technology Innovation and Regional Economic Development*. Washington, D.C.: Author. ED 251 295. 174 pp. MF–$1.07; PC–$16.36.

"University of Rochester Cancels Admission of Employee of a Kodak Competitor." 9 September 1987. *Chronicle of Higher Education* 34 (2): 1.

Van Pattee, Frank. 1973. *The Impact of Higher Education on the Economy of New Hampshire*. Durham: Univ. of New Hampshire.

Varrin, Robert, and Diane Kukich. 1985. "Guidelines for Industry-Sponsored Research at Universities." *Science* 227 (4685): 385–88.

Walker, Virginia L., and Werner Lowenthal. 1981. "Perceptions of Undergraduate Students toward Continuing Education." *American Journal of Pharmaceutical Education* 45 (3): 268–70.

Watkins, Charles B. 1985. *Programs for Innovative Technical Research in State Strategies for Economic Development*. Washington, D.C.: National Governors' Association, Center for Policy Research and Analysis.

Webster, David. 1986. *Academic Quality Rankings of American Colleges and Universities*. Springfield, Ill.: Charles C. Thomas.

Weiner, Charles. 1982. "Relations of Science, Government, and Industry: The Case of Recombinant DNA." In *Science, Technology, and the Issues of the Eighties: Policy Outlook*, edited by Albert H. Teich and Ray Thornton. Boulder, Colo.: Westview Press.

Williams, Bruce. 1986. "The Direct and Indirect Role of Higher Education in Industrial Innovations: What Should We Expect?" *Minerva* 24 (293): 145–71.

Winkler, Henry R. 1982. "Education and Business Prospering Together: Methods Which Work in the Collaborative Process." Paper presented to the American Council on Education, October. ED 235 356. 8 pp. MF–$1.07; PC–$3.85.

Wofsy, Leon. 1986. "Biotechnology and the University." *Journal of Higher Education* 57 (5): 477–92.

Zinser, Elizabeth A. June 1982. "Industry-Academia Relationships in Research and Innovation: The Case of Molecular Biology." Master's thesis, Sloan School of Management, Massachusetts Institute of Technology.

INDEX

C

Instruction
    adaptations, 15
    cost to, 57
    environment, 65
    mission, 64–68
    -related liaisons, 32–33
Intellectual property rights, 48, 63–64
Intrainstitutional locations, 35–36
Inventions, 63

J
Japan, 3, 6
Job training, 33, 69
Johns Hopkins University, 75

K
Korea, 3

L
Lag time, 46
Land-grant institutions
    creation, 1
    public service, 68
    social/economic responsiveness, 4
Leadership, 44–45, 50
Legal issues, 48–49
Legislation as motivator, 19
Liaisons (see Industry-university relationships)
Liberal arts, 73
Limited partnerships, 10
Loans: equipment, 27
Location, 34–36, 38

M
Management
    issues, 55–56
    styles, 46
Massachusetts Institute of Technology, 25, 28, 67, 75, 86
Methods of operation, 46
Michigan Research Corporation, 39
Microelectronics, 61
Mission
    academic, 45–46
    distinctiveness, 87–88, 90
    instruction and advising, 64–68

research and scholarship, 58–64
service, 4, 68–70
Monsanto Corporation, 25, 62, 78
Morrill Act of 1862, 1,4
Motivating factors
economic development, 19–20
faculty and students, 22–23
human capital, 20
innovation, 21
product development, 21
public relations, 23
reputation/prestige, 21, 23
resources, 20–22

N

National Science Board, 66
National Science Foundation
creation, 2
Engineering Research Centers, 6, 13, 19, 28
impact assessment, 77
National Technological University, 8
Needs overlap, 43–44
Negotiation: academic, 90
"New alliances," 22
Nonprofit organizations: advocacy, 16

O

Objectives, 15–17
Operational success, 49–55
Organizational structure, 50–51
Organized research units (ORU), 35
ORU (see Organized research units)

P

Pajaro Dunes conference, 71
Patent and Trademark Amendments of 1980, 48
Patents, 6, 48, 63, 80
Pennsylvania State University, 79
Personnel attitudes, 46–47
Policies, 51
Political agendas, 13–18
Prestige, 23
Product development
collegiate reward structure, 53
industry emphasis, 3, 21, 26, 45

Product line, 43
Productivity, 63
Professional development, 39–40
Program strengthening, 60
Proprietary institutions
     faculty from industry, 65
     industry liaisons, 29
Proprietary rights, 45, 55–56, 62, 66
Proximity (see also Location), 42
Public relations, 23
public service mission, 4, 68–70
Publications
     numbers of, 63
     restrictions on, 45, 62
Purchasing agreements, 26–27

Q

Quality decline in education, 5

R

Rand Graduate Institute, 8
Recruitment/retention of faculty/students, 22–23, 65, 80
Regional employment, 54, 82
Release time, 67
Remediation, 34
Reputation: corporate, 21
Research and development
     complexity, 20
     corporate strength, 43
     funds, 28
Research
     academic mission, 58–64
     agreements, 25–26, 37, 38, 72–73, 80, 86
     applied, 3, 46
     basic, 3, 22, 45, 46
     basic vs. applied, 62
     centers/institutes, 38
     contracts, 32
     cooperative projects, 38
     costs, 22
     facilities, 21
     federal investment, 19
     lag time, 46
     parks, 39
     structure, 72–73
     topic selection, 61

ASHE-ERIC HIGHER EDUCATION REPORTS

Since 1983, the Association for the Study of Higher Education (ASHE) and the ERIC Clearinghouse on Higher Education, a sponsored project of the School of Education and Human Development at the George Washington University, have cosponsored the ASHE-ERIC Higher Education Report series. The 1988 series is the seventeenth overall, with the American Association for Higher Education having served as cosponsor before 1983.

Each monograph is the definitive analysis of a tough higher education problem, based on thorough research of pertinent literature and institutional experiences. After topics are identified by a national survey, noted practitioners and scholars write the reports, with experts reviewing each manuscript before publication.

Eight monographs (10 monographs before 1985) in the ASHE-ERIC Higher Education Report series are published each year, available individually or by subscription. Subscription to eight issues is $60 regular; $50 for members of AERA, AAHE, and AIR; $40 for members of ASHE (add $10.00 for postage outside the United States).

Prices for single copies, including 4th class postage and handling, are $15.00 regular and $11.25 for members of AERA, AAHE, AIR, and ASHE ($10.00 regular and $7.50 for members for 1985 to 1987 reports, $7.50 regular and $6.00 for members for 1983 and 1984 reports, $6.50 regular and $5.00 for members for reports published before 1983). If faster postage is desired for U.S. and Canadian orders, add $1.00 for each publication ordered; overseas, add $5.00. For VISA and MasterCard payments, include card number, expiration date, and signature. Orders under $25 must be prepaid. Bulk discounts are available on orders of 15 or more reports (not applicable to subscriptions). Order from the Publications Department, ASHE-ERIC Higher Education Reports, The George Washington University, One Dupont Circle, Suite 630, Washington, D.C. 20036-1183, or phone us at 202/296-2597. Write for a publications list of all the Higher Education Reports available.

1988 ASHE-ERIC Higher Education Reports

1. The Invisible Tapestry: Culture in American Colleges and Universities
   George D. Kuh and Elizabeth J. Whitt

2. Critical Thinking: Theory, Research, Practice, and Possibilities
   Joanne Gainen Kurfiss

3. Developing Academic Programs: The Climate for Innovation
   Daniel T. Seymour

4. Peer Teaching: To Teach Is to Learn Twice
   Neal A. Whitman

5. Higher Education and State Governments: Renewed Partnership, Cooperation, or Competition?
   Edward R. Hines

6. Entrepreneurship and Higher Education: Lessons for Colleges, Universities, and Industry
   James S. Fairweather

1987 ASHE-ERIC Higher Education Reports

1. Incentive Early Retirement Programs for Faculty: Innovative Responses

to a Changing Environment
Jay L. Chronister and Thomas R. Kepple, Jr.

2. Working Effectively with Trustees: Building Cooperative Campus
Leadership
Barbara E. Taylor

3. Formal Recognition of Employer-Sponsored Instruction: Conflict and
Collegiality in Postsecondary Education
Nancy S. Nash and Elizabeth M. Hawthorne

4. Learning Styles: Implications for Improving Educational Practices
Charles S. Claxton and Patricia H. Murrell

5. Higher Education Leadership: Enhancing Skills through Professional
Development Programs
Sharon A. McDade

6. Higher Education and the Public Trust: Improving Stature in Colleges and
Universities
Richard L. Alfred and Julie Weissman

7. College Student Outcomes Assessment: A Talent Development
Perspective
Maryann Jacobi, Alexander Astin, and Frank Ayala, Jr.

8. Opportunity from Strength: Strategic Planning Clarified with Case
Examples
Robert G. Cope

1986 ASHE-ERIC Higher Education Reports

1. Post-tenure Faculty Evaluation: Threat or Opportunity?
Christine M. Licata

2. Blue Ribbon Commissions and Higher Education: Changing Academe
from the Outside
Janet R. Johnson and Lawrence R. Marcus

3. Responsive Professional Education: Balancing Outcomes and
Opportunities
Joan S. Stark, Malcolm A. Lowther, and Bonnie M.K. Hagerty

4. Increasing Students' Learning: A Faculty Guide to Reducing Stress
among Students
Neal A. Whitman, David C. Spendlove, and Claire H. Clark

5. Student Financial Aid and Women: Equity Dilemma?
Mary Moran

6. The Master's Degree: Tradition, Diversity, Innovation
Judith S. Glazer

7. The College, the Constitution, and the Consumer Student: Implications
for Policy and Practice
Robert M. Hendrickson and Annette Gibbs

8. Selecting College and University Personnel: The Quest and the Questions
Richard A. Kaplowitz

1985 ASHE-ERIC Higher Education Reports

1. Flexibility in Academic Staffing: Effective Policies and Practices
   Kenneth P. Mortimer, Marque Bagshaw, and Andrew T. Masland

2. Associations in Action: The Washington, D.C., Higher Education Community
   Harland G. Bloland

3. And on the Seventh Day: Faculty Consulting and Supplemental Income
   Carol M. Boyer and Darrell R. Lewis

4. Faculty Research Performance: Lessons from the Sciences and Social Sciences
   John W. Creswell

5. Academic Program Reviews: Institutional Approaches, Expectations, and Controversies
   Clifton F. Conrad and Richard F. Wilson

6. Students in Urban Settings: Achieving the Baccalaureate Degree
   Richard C. Richardson, Jr., and Louis W. Bender

7. Serving More Than Students: A Critical Need for College Student Personnel Services
   Peter H. Garland

8. Faculty Participation in Decision Making: Necessity or Luxury?
   Carol E. Floyd

1984 ASHE-ERIC Higher Education Reports

1. Adult Learning: State Policies and Institutional Practices
   K. Patricia Cross and Anne-Marie McCartan

2. Student Stress: Effects and Solutions
   Neal A. Whitman, David C. Spendlove, and Claire H. Clark

3. Part-time Faculty: Higher Education at a Crossroads
   Judith M. Gappa

4. Sex Discrimination Law in Higher Education: The Lessons of the Past Decade
   J. Ralph Lindgren, Patti T. Ota, Perry A. Zirkel, and Nan Van Gieson

5. Faculty Freedoms and Institutional Accountability: Interactions and Conflicts
   Steven G. Olswang and Barbara A. Lee

6. The High-Technology Connection: Academic/Industrial Cooperation for Economic Growth
   Lynn G. Johnson

7. Employee Educational Programs: Implications for Industry and Higher Education
   Suzanne W. Morse

8. Academic Libraries: The Changing Knowledge Centers of Colleges and Universities
   Barbara B. Moran

9. Futures Research and the Strategic Planning Process: Implications for

Higher Education
James L. Morrison, William L. Renfro, and Wayne I. Boucher

10. Faculty Workload: Research, Theory, and Interpretation
Harold E. Yuker

1983 ASHE-ERIC Higher Education Reports

1. The Path to Excellence: Quality Assurance in Higher Education
Laurence R. Marcus, Anita O. Leone, and Edward D. Goldberg

2. Faculty Recruitment, Retention, and Fair Employment: Obligations and Opportunities
John S. Waggaman

3. Meeting the Challenges: Developing Faculty Careers*
Michael C. T. Brookes and Katherine L. German

4. Raising Academic Standards: A Guide to Learning Improvement
Ruth Talbott Keimig

5. Serving Learners at a Distance: A Guide to Program Practices
Charles E. Feasley

6. Competence, Admissions, and Articulation: Returning to the Basics in Higher Education
Jean L. Preer

7. Public Service in Higher Education: Practices and Priorities
Patricia H. Crosson

8. Academic Employment and Retrenchment: Judicial Review and Administrative Action
Robert M. Hendrickson and Barbara A. Lee

9. Burnout: The New Academic Disease*
Winifred Albizu Meléndez and Rafael M. de Guzmán

10. Academic Workplace: New Demands, Heightened Tensions
Ann E. Austin and Zelda F. Gamson

*Out-of-print. Available through EDRS.

Media Center (Library)
ELIZABETHTOWN COMMUNITY COLLEGE
Elizabethtown, KY 42701

Order Form

QUANTITY   AMOUNT

_____ Please enter my subscription to the 1988 ASHE-ERIC
Higher Education Reports at $60.00, 50% off the cover
price, beginning with Report 1, 1988.

_____ Ple
Hig
pric

_____ Ou

Individual
1988 and
1985 to 19

Book rate
For fast U.
Outside U.
For air ma
All orders

15730

LB
2305
.E220
1988

QUANTIT
_____ Re
_____ Re
_____ Re

Please chec

☐ Check en
☐ Purchase
☐ Charge m

Expiration date _____

Name _____

Title _____

Institution _____

Address _____

City _____

Phone _____

DATE DUE

WITHDRAWN

ALL ORDERS SHOULD BE SENT TO:
ASHE-ERIC Higher Education Reports
The George Washington University
One Dupont Circle, Suite 630, Dept. RC
Washington, DC 20036-1183
Phone: 202/296-2597